Golden Nib
Teen Nib
Winners
2020

THE VIRGINIA WRITERS CLUB

Virginia Writers Club © 2020
P.O. Box 586
Moneta, VA 24121

John A. Nicolay, Ph.D., Editor
"The Golden Nib Teen Nib Winners 2020"

ISBN 9798563220867

https://www.virginiawritersclub.org/chapters

Chapters

Appalachian Authors Guild
Blue Ridge Writers
Chesapeake Bay Writers
Hampton Roads
Hanover Writers
Northern Virginia
Richmond
Riverside Writers
Valley Writers
Write by the Rails

Cover design "Blue Ridge Mountains"
by Leslie Truex
Image public domain, National Park Service

Price $7.50

Table of Contents

Poetry

Fiction

Nonfiction

Teen Nib (poetry, fiction, nonfiction awards)

Authors from left Lillian Lam, Gus Augustin, Patience Wallace, Autumn Ryan, and Cara J. Hadden.

Teen Nib 2020
Virginia Writers Club

The Virginia Writers Club
Fostering the art, craft, business, and advocacy of the literary arts throughout the Commonwealth.

Preface

The Commonwealth of Virginia had already produced many celebrated writers, including Edgar Allan Poe and Willa Cather, before James Branch Cabell, Ellen Glasgow, and other Virginia writers met for tea and formed the Virginia Writers Club in 1918. Since then, The Virginia Writers Club, Inc (VWC) has fostered the art, craft, business, and advocacy of the literary arts throughout the commonwealth. Former president, Samuel T. Schroetter, Jr (1916-1997), summed up the club's significance when he said:

Perhaps the greatest attraction, value, and potential of the Club is bringing together writers of various sorts...poets, fiction writers, essayists, scholars, journalists, editors, and a scattering of specialty, technical, and publicity writers. Writers in different disciplines and from different localities get to know each other, to compare, exchange, and share experiences; well-known authors meet their most devoted and understanding admirers, reviewers, and promoters; fledgling and flagged craftsmen meet and learn from expert practitioners, through programs and conversation. A poetry society, a historical association, an organization of women, black, Christian or Jewish writers, a purely local group does have the advantage of focus, but a more general writers' club has that of breadth and interchange.

Over the last one-hundred and two years, the club has expanded to ten chapters and three subchapters, where much of the programing for writers occurs. Many of the chapters offer regular critique groups and workshops. Some offer yearly retreats, while others host a yearly bookfair, and one runs its own successful podcast.

At the state level, VWC offers a variety of resources to assist writers, including grants to support chapter programming, a yearly writers symposium, an academic scholarship, and an expanding library of online resources and tools to help Virginia writers achieve their goals. Even during the challenging times of a global pandemic, VWC continues to support its members and chapters, and seek ways to expand its reach to Virginia writers.

In 2005, VWC created the Golden Nib writing contest to celebrate and recognize the talent in the organization. The first tier of the contest occurs at the chapter level where entries in the categories of poetry, nonfiction, and fiction are judged. We then send the winners of each category to the second tier, the state level, for judging.

This year, VWC re-booted its Teen Nib Contest to support and celebrate young writers in the commonwealth. High schoolers from across the state submitted their works in poetry, nonfiction, and fiction.

VWC is pleased to present this anthology of Golden Nib and Teen Nib 2020 submissions and winners. These works represent the continued depth and diversity in the club as celebrated by Samuel T. Schroetter, Jr's statement.

This anthology is dedicated to all past and present VWC members, and all its supporters who help make it a vibrant writing community.

Leslie Truex, President Virginia Writers Club

Note from the Editor

This collection is a first among many for the Virginia Writers Club. The Golden Nib contest provides recognition to members of the ten local chapters. Each genre could have ten submissions out of which three are placed, 1st, 2nd, and 3rd. Winning entries are posted on the VWC's website.

But all submissions are winners in their own rights. This publication celebrates all chapters that took part and includes the non-chapter affiliated high school "Teen Nib". This is a separate contest.

The Board of Governors agrees that we need to celebrate our writers, and to give them voice as a membership benefit. And here you are, in hand, the first of many.

Because the discussion to print this collection followed the posting of Golden Nib requirements, two participants had other commitments for their work and could not be included. One chapter could not take part.

Last note, illustrations enrich a publication by providing points of interest or hooks. It is my preference to fill half-page white space with an illustration. I worked with the authors to get these correct. Source credits for images are at the end of each section.

Contact me anytime.

Editor, John A Nicolay
VWCjournal@gmail.com? For Twitter **@VWCJournal**

Poetry

Let Her Go by Sarah Collins Honenberger
inspired by the oil painting 'Repose' by Dominic Avant

First Place

Let her go if she wants.
The sun, the shadows are her continent.
Unbroken skin and black as uncut jade,
she waits, but will not beg
for what was hers once and will again
be hers alone. You must not bind those hands,
fine-boned, unbloodied, and so regal.

Nefertiti called her out and yet
she did not bend, only let the moon drift on
without her. Unspoken dreams and
time like the lost pharaohs
braid up the fairest and bury them deep.
You cannot cure that
destruction, only
raise the cry, sound the
horn,
order your cities to bow
down and
she will again
be queen.

Repose by Dominic Avant

And the *Chicos* Come by Esther Whitman Johnson
Valley Chapter
After *Enrique's Journey* by Sonia Nazario

Second Place

Chicos come
by the thousands—from Honduras,
Mexico, El Salvador—
searching for Mama, gone
before her child's grown his wings.

Seeking more for those left behind,
Mama slaves for *gringas*, scrubbing floors,
tending children not her own —
back sore, exhausted to her bones,
spirit broken in the Land of Opportunity.

She visits Western Union,
sends money home—for food,
clothing, shoes to make him proud
strutting through the *barrio*.
On Mother's Day she phones and cries.

Then
the *chicos* come,
young as nine or ten,
ragged clothes on their backs,
phone numbers penned on their skin.

The *chicos* come
hopping trains, hacking jungle,

climbing mountains, swimming
the Rio Grande—starved, beaten,
raped—prey for roving gangs

who take their clothes, throw them naked
from the train, where doors are slammed
and they are shamed
as *migrants, beggars, filthy thieves.*

The *chicos* come, dying, maimed,
losing legs to the train, captured
at the line, deported time after time,
sneaking back again to the land
of dreams that promises everything
but delivers only pain.

Still, the *chicos* come

Graveyards of the Living by Judy Whitehill Witt
Richmond Chapter

Third Place

Spines grip ribs of paper;
nerves stitch bodies of work.

Whitman bestows his soul –
he waits for us, bound
in sheaves of seasoned grass.
His DNA does not arrest,
but rests in veins of ink.

Engraving's more for Poe,
yet beneath his icy stone
thrums a tell-tale heart
never to be silenced,
eager to be heard again,
quiet nevermore.

Frost's way leads on to way;
though his path diverged,
he keeps his promise still.
Despite miles dark and deep,
ages hence, he's here.
Every graveyard speaks,
its dwellers never dead,
circulating on the breath
of turning earth, exhaling
at peak of searing brilliance,

inspiring, birthing more,
ever more libraries.

God's Cathedral by John L. Dutton, II
Write by the Rails Chapter

God's Cathedral was not made by man's hand,
It was made by the wind, the sea, the sand, and the soil.
There is no time table or tools required to build this house
of worship,
The only item required to raise this holy house is time.
Time's toolbox cannot be contained!
Thunder, lightning, wind, rain, surf, sand, snow, and hail -
Tools that toil the earth constantly crafting its beauty.
No one who worships here wears their Sunday best or waits
for the Sabbath.
No offering is collected -
The only tribute paid is the sweat running down one's back

and the solace one finds in contemplation after challenging
oneself to venture outside.
The choir consists of waves breaking upon the shore.
The creatures chirp and chatter the sermon endlessly.
The breeze rejuvenates the congregation
who, when ready, rise to continue onward deeper into the
forest.

The May Forest by Jennifer Gaden
Blue Ridge Writers

The May forest is like no other -
all of its own.
Not what Robert Frost said -
"Natures first green is gold"
when April rays penetrate the branches
with the strong fingers of a midwife,
coaxing and kneading the fleshy buds
to unfold fully. But then he said -
"Nothing Gold Can Stay."

In May the leaves are newborn
fresh as the first breath of dawn,
baptized by showers and bird song.
Tear drops brought by the rain
hover at the tips -
a rainbow in a globe.

At the bottom of the leaf infused sea
fists of little ferns uncurl,
encircled by their own dry bones,
yielding slowly, slowly
their riches to the soil.

By June there is a change.
The green is strong, confident,
not innocent,
indulgent in the fecundity
of the earth.

I Didn't Know by Harry Heckel
Hanover Chapter

I wanted to tell you that
I didn't know
About diapers, rattles
Or how the car seat latches
I wasn't ready
For long nights, spit rags
Or playpens and walkers
I didn't know
So much about trains
Or the best color crayons
I wasn't ready
To forget your bear
Or wipe away your tears
I didn't know
If time out would help
Or if a hug was best
I didn't know
First grade was scary
And making friends so hard
I wasn't ready
For our school play star
Or no more bedtime stories
I didn't know
All cellphones could do
Or how to teach driving
I wasn't ready
For that first heartbreak
Or a camp for two weeks

I didn't know
That you spoke so well
Or how proud I could feel
I wasn't ready
When you crossed that stage
And tossed your cap so high
I didn't know
How hard it would be
To pack up your things
And drive you to the dorm
I wasn't ready
For the empty house
Or the quiet evenings
I don't know
What we used to do
But the one thing that's true -
We will always love you.

No Reason to Rest by Devin Reese
Northern Virginia Chapter

If the cost is waking startled from the next prick
    of my damned WHITE skin,
        I'd rather not rest.

The anticipation keeps me alert.
    Each prick is a bias,
    each bias wrapped in a wail,
    each wail a torrent
    that stirs my blood humors to circulate.
The biases spread to limbs,
    changing resting synapses to alarm circuits.

The racial biases were not hidden inside me,
rather mockingly just in view.
    Here a microaggression tucked into a nook,
    there a racial slur hanging off a branch,
    in the soil a scattering of false assumptions about
    brains and bodies and intentions,
all shrouded in a sorrowful mist
of generations of the lynched and disenfranchised.

I missed the biases before, though
I've walked this path a thousand times.
Now each one whispers urgently, and
I cannot quite ignore their voices, yet
strain to understand what they are telling me.

They ask me to listen and listen again,
for they are not speaking softly they claim, but
yelling out, standing on the pyramid of generations
of black people piled up like burnt and wasted timbers.

Race-blind is my defense, for I used to dream of people
who all looked alike –
      same skin color,
      same body,
      to be judged on their thoughts alone.
But now, race-blind makes a flimsy, awkward shield.
To choose blindness is to negate what should be seen,
to claim indifference to color in favor of more darkness.

My daughter tried to explain, dark eyes flashing
in her pale face, that Black Lives Matter is not about us.
We are all guilty and don't deserve to state our case again.
      It is THEIR time, she said,
      and brandished her Black Lives Matter signs,
      bobbing resolutely through the crowds
      of black and brown faces.

But, not until my oldest friend, who I had
      never seen as BLACK,
told me that I had 40 years ago called her Nigger-woman,
did I despair that I know nothing about myself and bias,
and have everything to learn and be humbled by,
about the experience of being black,
in America.

Still Thinking by Ellen Myatt
Appalachian Authors Guild

Years ago
when you sent
that pen and ink
it made me think.

Images darker
than Bible black
brought back
bits of our dark youth.

Yet, never did I know
the depth those times
would go
and hide within you.

You carried them
in a duffle bag
to your barracks in 1974
this side of the Berlin Wall.

You were so young
with wayward friends
I was at one end of life
working toward another.

Remember – I was your sister,
not your mother
I was sure it was a
good decision to let you go.

Yet, when you sent
that pen and ink
it made me think
Otherwise.

Beer bottles, Bicycle® cards
dice and money
floated above
the helmets of men without faces.

All that black in negative space
made me wonder
what you were
saying without words.

Was the pen and ink
to make me think
the cold war could be
ending?

Did you intend to show
what we would later
come to know
as history?

Years have passed
yet *this* pen and ink
still makes me think
of your talent dark and raw.

Weathering Grief by Elizabeth Spencer Spragins
Riverside Chapter

daylight takes her leave
and packs away her paintings—
the ache of evening
fingers each beloved rock
lined by centuries of loss

~Grand Canyon National Park, Arizona

Notes on images

Page 1, Creative Commons License 2.0

Page 2, Repose by Dominic Avant dominicavant.com. Permission of the artist. Fair use

Page 4, Courtesy of NPR, fair use

Page 5, Derivative, images public domain

Page 6, "Behold the lilies of the field" by Radames M is licensed under CC BY-NC-SA 2.0

Page 9, Derivative, figure Creative Commons license 2.0

Page 34, Creative Commons license 2.0

Fiction

Not Today by Sandra Roslan
Hanover Chapter

First Place

The chill engulfed me.

"Jonah!" I rubbed the goosebumps on my arms. "Personal space! How many times have I told you not to walk through me?"

"You were in my way."

"You're a freaking ghost! Go around me, walk through the damn furniture instead!"

Jonah chuckled, and this time a warm breeze brushed by me. "Sometimes I just want to make sure I have your attention."

"Well, what do you want?"

"I'm bored."

"Not my problem, I'm not here to entertain you."

"Sure you are. I saved your soul, so when I'm bored you have to amuse me with your charming wit."

"Amuse this," I said, giving him the finger.

Yes, I'm grateful Jonah kept my spirit from moving on, but that didn't mean I was going to cater to his whims every time he played the "I saved your soul" card.

No other ghosts spoke to me. When I asked Jonah why, he explained as my spirit guide, he could communicate with me effortlessly. Spirits expend a lot of energy talking to anyone other than the specific people they are attached to, and most thought it wasn't worth it, so I likely wouldn't be friends with any other ghosts. I told him he was more than enough ghost for me and of course, he took that as a compliment.

Years ago, I went swimming with friends. While in the ocean, a huge waved slammed into me, forced me under, and bounced my head off the ocean floor.

My next recollection was a bright hallway, with

doors dotting the corridor. The last door was ajar and emitting a soft glow I was drawn to. I walked down the hall and I could hear voices from the open door. No words, only a collective buzz, like when I eavesdropped on the adults as a kid during family gatherings. I was passing the last door before the one I found I mentally referred to as *mine* when a distinct voice cut through the friendly hum.

"Nope, not today!" I was socked in the chest hard enough to catapult me through the door I was closest to. I woke up hacking out sea water with my chest throbbing. Later, I found out when my friends realized what happened, they hauled me out of the ocean and started life-saving measures.

That's how I met Jonah, and since then, he'd never left. He kept talking to me. A lot. At first, I assumed something was wrong, causing me to hear voices. Well, *a* voice. I saw psychiatrists, neurologists, and a hypnotherapist. I even consulted a priest. After many appointments, tests, and sessions, they came to the same conclusions. I wasn't crazy. I didn't have brain damage. I wasn't having a religious epiphany.

Next, I tried ignoring Jonah, hoping he would go away. He didn't. I finally faced the fact I was stuck with him and we settled into a somewhat amicable existence.

Jonah had the 411 on the spirits around us. Turns out, the afterlife is a hotbed of gossip, which comes in handy when you decide to become a private investigator. With Jonah's finger on the pulse, if you will, of the dead and my good instincts we rented a small storefront, hung a shingle, and opened *Reesa Montgomery Investigations.* And, yes, Jonah did complain about his name missing from the sign.

The phone rang, and the display lit up as my friend, Detective Tom Lansing calling. Tom didn't know about Jonah. He'd been at the beach the day of the accident and often joked that ever since I had psychic powers. Since I proved helpful when he needed me, he didn't question it.

"Hi, Tom."

"Reesa, hey. There's a little girl missing in Red Top. We're not getting anywhere with what we have." A beat. "I was hoping..."

I tapped the speaker button. "Give me the details."

"Name's Lindley Ogden, four years old, forty pounds, red hair, green eyes. Last seen at approximately 7:30 pm when her parents put her to bed. No signs of forced entry. Goes to pre-school a couple times a week. We've talked to everybody that had regular contact with the kid but no leads so far."

My heart clenched as I jotted down the addresses he gave me and told him I'd be in touch.

When I hung up, Jonah said, "She's not dead, at least not yet." His last words being the morbid possibility I hoped to avoid.

I arrived at the Ogden's with Jonah in tow. Ringing the bell sparked a cacophony of barking from a pack of dogs. Through the door I heard someone say, "Enough, Barney." The barking dropped in volume until it tapered off to silence. When the door opened, a lone beagle stood beside the couple who confirmed they were Jim and Stephanie Ogden.

They brought me through their house into the kitchen.

Once seated, Stephanie blinked puffy eyes at me while Jim twisted his red hair into knots. A few seconds later, Mr. Ogden's eyes began to leak tears. He said, "I thought I heard a noise last night after we put Lindley to bed, but I figured it was our dog, so I went back to sleep." Barney looked woefully at me from a bed in the corner, like he was sorry it wasn't him too.

"Who does that?" he continued, his voice breaking. "What kind of man lets someone come into their house and take their child? I should've checked..."

His wife tried to comfort him, and he shrugged her off. "It's not your fault, Jim. I thought it was Barney too."

Sitting across from the distraught couple, I felt guilt coming off them in waves. I sympathized but listening to them blame themselves wasn't helping. I looked at the dog in the corner. He'd had no reaction to whoever entered the home. Between that and no signs of forced entry, it looked like someone familiar to the family abducted the child.

Jonah was quiet, and I knew he was looking around the house to see what he could find. I asked to see Lindley's room. It was a typical kid's room with toys and books. The cheerful wallpaper beamed unicorns and rainbows. Her parents told me that Lindley's favorite stuffed animal, a green bear, was also missing.

I asked for a list of anyone the family might have had contact with recently. They jotted down repairmen, their book club members, their weekly housekeeper for the last year, and a few babysitters.

As I was leaving, Mr. Ogden touched my shoulder, "Please find our daughter." His weepy eyes locked with mine in a plea I hoped to fulfill. His wife stood behind him, staring at me with the same intensity.

I was frozen, torn between promising false hope and by nature wanting to alleviate their pain. I felt my ear tickle, a sign I'd grown used to over the years, identifying that Jonah was near and about to speak. "Tell them you'll do your best. It's okay to give them hope." Ironically, he was always better with the living than me.

I looked at the parents, "I promise I'll do my best. I'll be in touch as soon as I know something. Please call if you think of anything else. Even the smallest detail could be important."

Two hours later, after making dozens of calls, I still didn't know much more than when I started. The office was quiet without Jonah's incessant chatter and our usual banter. While I had been working on the earthbound side of things, he contacted the We R Dead hotline on the other side.

I stood up for a stretch. The notepad on my desk was full of scribbles, but none of them contained the answer I was seeking.

"Jonah?" Nothing. I could get his attention by opening my mind and casting out for him, but I knew he was busy, so I let him be.

I pulled a water bottle from the mini-fridge and sat back down, rereading all the notes I had made.

The pre-school teacher was young and nervous when we spoke, getting defensive when I asked if she had noticed anyone lurking around when the children played outside. She acted like I accused her of neglecting the kids.

The next notes were on a roofer named Brandon Evans. I hadn't been able to get in touch with him, but I found his Facebook page. He was well built and had a crooked smile. He worked at the Ogden's house a few months ago. I contacted some clients he mentioned under the guise of getting references for a roofing job, and nobody had anything bad to say about him. He was a nice dude, on time, did a good job.

Another quick search revealed he had a long record of petty crimes that dried up five years ago, around the time he got married. As I continued scrolling backwards through his timeline, I found several rants he directed towards an adoption agency. From his posts, I pieced together he and his wife had been turned down by the agency after they had already been promised a child.

Then we had Sharon McAvoy, the housekeeper. I found her on social media too. While the roofer's page oozed vitriol, hers spewed cheerfulness. Lots of inspirational memes and mantras for positive energy. Her Instagram told me she was currently in the Bahamas sipping Mai Tais. She'd left last week on a cruise and wouldn't be home for a while, according to a post from yesterday hashtagged #onemoreweekinparadise. Other pictures showed her poolside on the ship, standing beside the "Welcome to Freeport" sign, and snorkeling with sea life. Today's post was of a parasailing dock, hashtagged #tomorrow with happy emojis.

I fired up my Finder app (which may or may not skirt the edges of legality) and searched her name. The app told me the ship's manifest had her checking in a week ago and her credit card had recent transactions at several shops located in Freeport and the surrounding areas.

Sighing, I leaned back in my chair, threading my fingers together behind my head.

"Think, think, think," I said to myself, tapping with each utterance, hoping I would rattle a new idea loose.

"Quit that, it's bad for your brain," Jonah said from somewhere behind me, startling me so bad I knocked over my water.

"You're bad for my brain," I muttered, sopping up the mess with napkins.

"I heard that," he said. I rolled my eyes.

"I haven't found anything yet," I told him. "You?"

"Nope. I checked with Poppy at the railroad, Slinger in the trailer park, and Guppy over by the waterfront. They're the biggest gossips of the afterlife. If they don't know it, it's not worth knowing."

Ghosts went by nicknames in the afterlife. Usually it was a hint to the way they died. I'd tried to find out what Jonah used but much like many other details about himself, he never told me. I had no idea when or where he lived and died or any information about his family.

I decided to get some lunch and hopefully kick-start my brain. Time was ticking, and I was getting bummed out. Jonah said he would keep trying to make connections while I was gone.

I went to a nearby burger place and hit the drive

thru. As I pulled away from the window, my cellphone rang so I swung into a deserted space in the lot.

I answered to Mrs. Ogden talking so fast I could barely understand her. I focused on her words. "Jim found a hammer under Lindley's window." There was a rustle as Jim took the phone.

"It had the logo of the roofing company we hired months ago! It was in the mulch, almost covered up! It belonged to Brandon Evans! I'm going to kill that son of a bitch!"

My mind clicked back to the Facebook page I had looked at earlier and the rants about the unfairness of the adoption process.

"We called that detective. Lansing. They're sending someone to track down the bastard right now."

"I'm heading to your house," I said.

I disconnected our call, my burger forgotten. I needed Jonah. I relaxed as much as possible, cleared my mind and concentrated. I silently reached out to him.

A few seconds passed. "I'm here."

On the way to the Ogden's I recapped the call for him. My theory was, Brandon saw Lindley when he was working on the house, and he was so fed up with the adoption process he decided that she would make the perfect addition to his family. He had probably been planning the kidnapping for months. He could've stolen a spare key while he was there. One thing bothered me. The dog. He was a nervous sort that made a fuss when people came to the house he didn't know.

Police were at the Ogden's and the couple was talking to a uni in the yard when I pulled up. Barney barked at the top of his lungs, watching the commotion from the window.

Jonah spoke, "There's weird energy here. Like a spirit is trying to come through."

My heart plummeted. "Is it Lindley?"

Silence. Then, "No."

I breathed a sigh of relief.

"I can't get a read on them. The pull is coming from the house."

The Ogdens finished with the cop and motioned me toward them. Local news crews were setting up across the street.

"Come on," Mrs. Ogden said. "Let's get inside before they come over here to grab their evening soundbite. Vultures, the lot of them."

Barney ran to us when we entered the door, still barking for all he was worth. "Hush," Jim commanded, but the hound kept going. Jim squatted down to soothe the animal. "It's okay buddy, all these strangers have you wound up, I know." Barney settled at his master's touch.

As we entered the kitchen, I saw that the under-sink cabinet was open with cleaning supplies on the floor in disarray. Stephanie looked at the mess. "That latch must be coming loose. That's been popping open all day." She put the items away while I sat at the table with Mr. Ogden.

The dog, now quiet, trotted over and sniffed me. He backed away and sat on his bed.

"Don't take it personally, he's funny with strangers," Stephanie said, placing in front of me a cup of coffee I didn't really want.

"Thanks. How do you think Brandon got past him without being barked at?" I asked, sipping the coffee. It needed sugar.

"That's the thing. Every now and then he'll take to someone, and Brandon was one of those people. It made me like the man, seeing how he was with Barney, but now..." Jim trailed off, and I could only imagine what he was thinking.

"Why our daughter?" Stephanie asked, looking to me.

I started speaking to be interrupted by a creak and a

loud thump. The cabinet across the kitchen had swung open again and some spray cleaner fell out.

"Damn," Stephanie said. "I know I put that in there so it couldn't fall out again."

As she got up Jim said, "Steph, just leave it."

"No, I'll get it," she said. I wondered if the normalcy of cleaning up a small mess comforted her and gave her something else to concentrate on for a moment.

My ear tickled. "That feeling... it's strongest in here."

I rubbed my ear to make the tingle go away and to signal to Jonah that I heard him. I couldn't talk to him now unless I wanted the Ogdens to think I was bonkers.

Stephanie shut the cabinet and tested the latch to make sure it was securely fastened before coming to sit again.

I knew she still wanted an answer to her question, so I explained Brandon Evans and his wife wanted to adopt a child, but the agency turned them down.

Mr. Ogden's face grew as red as his hair while I talked, knuckles whitening around his coffee cup. Just when I thought the mug would crack, the cabinet sprang open again, this time ejecting two spray bottles and a dustpan so hard they bumped across the kitchen floor.

At the same time there was a rap on the door and Barney jumped up and started barking. Barney and Jim answered the door while Stephanie dug in a drawer for a flashlight, fretting about the possibility of mice.

Suddenly, Jonah yelled in my ear, "They finally came through!"

"Who?" I reactively yelled back, and Stephanie looked up.

"What?" she said.

"Oh, I was just clearing my throat," I covered. "May I use your bathroom?"

A few minutes later I was having a whispered

conversation with Jonah in the Ogden's bathroom. He finally connected with the spirit of a female teenager who died two years ago. He explained when souls have a rough transition, they are not able to communicate with other ghosts for a long time. This spirit was still learning to speak audibly but figured out how to manipulate objects. The dead teen was Talia McAvoy, daughter of the housekeeper, and she was doing her best to alert someone that her mother had Lindley.

I sprinted out of the bathroom and skidded into the kitchen. Stephanie sat at the table bawling while Jim slumped in the opposite chair, staring at nothing.

Jim's eyes slid to me, "He doesn't have her." His voice was flat, as though he was unable to even muster energy for inflection.

"It's Sharon. Your housekeeper," I said, dialing Tom's number.

I told him an edited version of Jonah's story, explaining I'd discovered an obituary for Talia, making me suspect Sharon.

I left the confused Ogdens in their kitchen and GPS'd my way to Sharon's house. I usually didn't get involved in this part, but today was an exception.

When I pulled up, Tom and several police cars were already there. Sharon was in the back of one of the patrol cars.

Sue, a policewoman I was familiar with from other cases, gestured me over. "She came quietly. The girl is in the house. Let's go get her."

I followed Sue through the house to a back room. Sue nudged the door open and we peeked in. I recognized the red headed child as Lindley. She sat at a kids-sized table, a colorful drawing in front of her. The tip of her tongue poked out as she examined the crayon choices before picking one. She looked up at us.

"Hi!" she said. Seeing the uniform Sue was

wearing, her eyebrows pulled together. "Am I in trouble?"

"No, not at all, sweetheart," Sue assured.

Lindley wasn't convinced, and her bottom lip quivered. I stepped forward, "My name's Reesa. That's a pretty picture you have there."

Her concerned face changed to a smile. "It's my house. There's the tree in the front yard and my dog Barney looking out the window." She had the faintest of lisps when she spoke.

"It's very nice," I told her.

Her green bear was beside her. "What's your friend's name?" I asked.

"Theodore," she said. "I'm glad Ms. Sharon let me bring him when she picked me up. She said Mommy and Daddy asked her to watch me, and he could keep me company."

"What else did you do while she's been taking care of you?"

"She read me a book and did all the animal voices. She's funny." She giggled. "I liked the hedgehog. And she made my favorite," her voice dropped to a conspiratorial whisper, "grilled cheese."

I grinned at her. "That's my favorite too."

"Ms. Reesa," she hesitated, "I'm having fun, but I miss Mommy and Daddy." Her little face sobered and her eyes dropped to her hands.

I squatted to her level. "You're going to see them soon. I promise."

After booking Sharon, Tom called and told me she admitted to planning the kidnapping for six months. She was tormented without her daughter, and she started to believe that she could raise Lindley as her own. She revived an old Instagram account and used pictures taken from a trip to the Bahamas years ago.

To strengthen her alibi, Sharon gifted the cruise ticket to a friend. She also gave her a credit card to buy souvenirs to bring back to her. She swore she wouldn't have hurt Lindley. A psychiatric evaluation was pending.

What a whirlwind of a day. I was tired, and I never did eat after abandoning my burger. I flipped on the closed sign and locked up the office behind me. As I drove home, my ear tingled. "You know my favorite show comes on tonight, so don't hog the TV."

"Jonah! Personal space! How many times have I told you, don't talk right in my ear if you don't have to?"

He chuckled.

Her green bear was beside her. "What's your friend's name?" I asked.

**The Dark Side of the Moon
by Sarah Collins Honenberger
Chesapeake Bay Writers**

Third Place

The day we buried my sister, the hydrangeas broadsided the yard like the original mushroom cloud itself. Not at all the tentative wavery way I remembered them drooping low when Krissy and I were kids. These hydrangeas struck at your heart, vociferous in their energy, inexplicable in their sudden profusion, a mystery that announced Krissy's absence when all I wanted was to pretend it was not so. Standing alone amidst those glowing orbs, I felt weak, short of breath, as if I might faint if I did not shield my eyes.

At that point, I had not been home for nine or ten years. But Krissy asked for me when the surgery failed. Called out for me by name.

On the phone, Mom had been livid. "The tumor is in her brain. They could not get it all. No drugs, they are out of options. It's just pain meds until, until ..." She gulped at the air. "One of her friends saw Paul in Minneapolis, and even after she told him all the gory details, he had nothing to say, not even that he was sorry. As if he barely knew her, as if they had never been married. Krissy still refuses to ask him to pay support for the girls."

When Mom took a breath, her bitterness lingered in the silence like the worst kind of eavesdropper. She had trouble telling me the rest. "The surgeon says it's a matter of days. Krissy wants you to come home."

What Mom did not say was even more obvious. I was just as bad as Paul. A job on the other side of the continent, rare phone calls, no holiday visits. Mom would never have asked me herself. Forgiveness is not her long suit. Losing me was an insult she worked at like an old sweater frayed at the sleeve. Losing Krissy would be the end of the world.

Still, I did not take her word for it. I called the hospital. Once I convinced the operator it was urgent, Carla Somerville, one of the ICU nurses, an old high school flame, confirmed it. Totally against regulations, but Carla had never refused me much. She knows I am not a total jerk. Sometimes I stumble onto the right thing.

When I was nineteen, I may have ripped out of small-town USA for all the wrong reasons. Jade Osborn was pregnant, though I am surer than not, it was not my baby. According to her she was sleeping with half the senior class. But Jade is not why I left.

Iraq was not in my future, the same as Joe College was not my alter ego. My father had opted out years earlier, and we had the same genes.

Out west, away from the small-town newspaper-clipping biddies who knew which bush I'd dumped my contraband coffee under on the way to middle school, I found a job running a hospital parking garage in Austin. Hourly pay without annual review and no one jumping on you for low production. At first, I mostly drank my earnings. It was not an original idea, but well-supported by my new friends, the people that avoid long conversations. After Texas, I tried Minneapolis, eventually settled in Oklahoma. Different town. Different parking garage. By then I had my five-year chip and a woman friend who did not ask for much beyond that.

I took up reading to fill the time. After I re-read Kipling and Conrad, I moved on to Tom Wolfe and Annie Proulx. In a good week—no one locking their keys in their car or backing into the brand-new SUV of some uppity doctor's wife—I could knock out two or three classics. The Top 100 books to read before you die. That was my mission. It was like watching the television static of the fifties, a constant numbing blur.

For three years the Oklahoma City library welcomed me, the best kind of family. No motion sensors sparked a late-night return, no disturbing questions, total anonymity. I was in love without being required to perform. Nothing to it but nod to the librarians and keep my voice down. Even I could not screw up that. For book suggestions, I used an online site. I read the reviews and rated their helpfulness, every bit as professional as a regular book critic. It was not responsibility I was running from.

In my infrequent calls home, Mom refused to talk to me. Krissy, though, acted like she was kind of proud of me. For making the break, for paying my own bills, for finding new friends with a horizon bigger than Podunk, VA. I might have laid it on a little thick, quoting Roth and Kerouac. When you only have one sister, it is hard not to want to make her happy.

When Krissy eloped with Paul, it saved me what would have been my first trip home after Dad's funeral. No money wasted on a wedding, clever girl.

Later the jerk left her with two girls. It made more sense for them to share Mom's house. I would have been in the way. With only Dad's railroad pension, Mom had to keep working. Krissy had enough to get by, to keep up the utilities and taxes. I sent money for birthdays and Christmas.

The tumor was a surprise. A goddamn shock. We are a rare family, no genetic history of cancer or heart disease. No weird extra-terrestrial radiation threatened the health of the MacIntyre family tree. No aquifer ran under the old neighborhood, and Mom could not afford a microwave. I am so effing healthy, little old ladies who do not even know me reach out to pinch my rosy cheeks.

Krissy's kids look the part too. They are cute, bouncy girls with brassy curls like their mom. She sent pictures to Oklahoma. Lots of pictures. They were her hobby. When I got to the waiting room, it was easy to recognize them. Six and five, wound around each other, bent over the Formica coffee table with a shared coloring book, their markers like confetti on the table and floor beside them. No hug for their Uncle Tim, but then they had never met me, and I had not sent photos east. Krissy's pictures of me from high school would not have been much help. I'd been a throwback to the draft dodgers of the sixties.

When Mom looked up through the ICU glass wall, she caught me staring through at Krissy. She lay white as a bride on that table, which was a bed, though there was nothing soft about it. *Tim*, Mom mouthed, and Krissy turned her head. At her smile, I bawled like a coed the morning after. Carla Somerville brought me a mask and gown, baby blue. She dressed me like a baby too, even kissed my cheek, then motioned for Mom to come out so I could go in.

Although that hardly seemed fair when I had been the one to stay away, I shut up when Carla pointed to the posted rules, right there by the door, inch high letters. *One visitor at a time.* What idiot hospital administrator promulgated that rule? To force dying people to rank their family at the one point in their lives when they may want to be surrounded by everyone they know and love. As hard as I'd worked to keep my distance, I understood that much about families.

There has never been any doubt in my mind that Krissy loved us all. Maybe I had not earned it, but when your only sister's dying you can't worry about that. That rule about visitors made me angry. Her girls were not even within eyesight, not holding her hand, not hearing her tell them how much she loved them. I wanted to carry them in—to hell with the rule—but Mom was adamant. She held my arm.

"It doesn't matter," she said. "They're too young to remember her, anyway. Nine is the earliest age when your memory can drag things back to the surface with any kind of clarity."

Nine, jeez, I had already kissed three girls by then and won the school record for the 500-yard dash and tried my first cigarette. Long before nine I had decided somewhere deep in my subconscious that Podunk would not claim me the way it had my father. It was small town gossip and despair that fired the rifle into his open mouth.

With that image from our basement still so close to the surface, I knew Mom was wrong about the age for remembering. Still, I decided it was not my call. Fine, I announced, we will leave the girls out of this.

The ICU cubicle was cozy and Krissy was relieved to see me. "The girls," she started, her voice thin, without the clear vibrato of energy I remembered.

Although I tried not to guess what was coming next, not even an escape artist like me would have argued back, not with all those busy machines and Mom taking sentry outside, her hand over her mouth and her eyes wide.

I took Krissy's hands. "It's okay, Kris. The girls are fine. Coloring together, good friends. They'll be fine."

"Mom's too old."

"Mom'll be fine too," I said, pretending to misunderstand while the glare of sunlight through the glass crashed around me with all that truth and justice glory, the right thing singing in my ears as loudly as the National Anthem. No way to ignore it.

"Tim, you have to stay."

"Sure, sure." Another easy promise, I was here, wasn't I? She hadn't defined a time. No strings attached for the wayward brother who embraced evasion, I had had lots of practice.

"You're not drinking?" The words spread pockets of warm air in the tiny room, invisible fingers on my face and arms. She'd always been blunt.

"Gave it up for Lent. Seven Lents ago."

She laughed, though the smile came and went so fast I almost missed it. I twisted back to the glass to see if Mom had caught it, a small hope burgeoning in my chest that forgiveness was possible. But she was gone. The space where she had radiated brainwaves of irritation with the entire situation, the cancer, the doctors, and especially my being inside and her being out. She would not believe me later about the smile.

"Have you finished reading everything in that Oklahoma library yet?" Krissy managed.

"You're still trying to convince me to move on."

"Please." But she failed at the 's' and slipped away from me. Her eyes murky with memories she was not sharing, her hands loosened, cooled.

When I realized she was done talking, I sat for a while inhaling the blend of her breathing and the machines, a hazy nocturne of regret and relief. I bent closer so as not to lose the rhythm. Let them all think we were deep in conversation. Soft light, comfortable chair, no more questions. I felt right at home. I had nowhere else I wanted or needed to be. It took me until the sun set, back lit gold and purple through the window blinds, until I could admit I had nowhere else to go.

Carla brought the papers to me, Krissy's election for no machines once she stopped breathing on her own, dated years earlier before any hint of the tumor, and her designation of me for custodian. Mom stayed away. I guessed, hoped she was busy with the girls and not overcome in some corner, fighting against her own despair. By the time the lines went flat I saw with an astonishing clarity that there was not anything in Oklahoma City worth retrieving, another hard truth I'd been avoiding. Carla let me stay with Krissy while the two nurses dealt with the empty hum, the cords, the mechanical indicia of life and death. Once they were done, with her hand on my elbow as if I had taken a terrible fall, Carla led me out of the glass cubicle.

Between sobs, Mom glared. "Great timing as always."

When I tried to hug her, she backed away.

"Go to hell," she said.

Carla kept pushing me forward, her other arm at my waist, until we were past and into the waiting room with its blooming carpet of colored markers.

I was struggling for a foothold. "Remember the scene in *A Streetcar Named Desire* when she says she's always relied on the kindness of strangers?" Swamped by long ago images of Krissy and me as kids, whispers across the dark hallway in the silent house, my feet stuck to the carpet.

Carla gripped my hand. "She's in a better place, Tim. No more pain."

"You know that for sure?"

"It's my job."

Was that it? It was easier to believe her. Or else the fight had just gone out of me. Ten years, maybe that was long enough.

Somehow the little girls figured out, without anyone saying anything, what had happened and who I was. They came running, wild tears and arms scrabbling. They burrowed into my arms as if it were the only safe place, the one thing they knew with certainty their mother had never stopped loving. Once they were quiet, I finally met Mom's eyes. The sting of that familiar coldness was tinged with something new. Regret, surprise, hope? As if she saw finally what Krissy knew about me that even I hadn't known.

"You take the girls home," she said. "I can't leave her."

I did not argue. I was not a complete novice. I had been through it with Dad. Going through the motions is what really matters. It avoids the kind of decisions a guy on the twelve-step program is not confident he can make on his own.

After the funeral, days later, after I'd moved the girls' twin beds into Krissy's old room and repeated the sleeping pill routine to Mom until she understood it, I finally had a minute to sit down and think. She was finishing the dishes, her face waxy and distant in the window's reflection, splinters of anger, shards of despair in her unfocused gaze at the blank window, the blank future. Or maybe into a past that was flickering and fading even as she groped for it to linger.

"I'm sorry to disrupt your life," she said.

"Oklahoma? That was an intermission."

She sat down across from me, wrapped her fingers around the coffee mug and stared at nothing. "When Krissy first got sick, it never occurred to me she'd die. It is not the natural order of things to bury a daughter. But Krissy knew. At least it seemed like she knew. She never cried, never ranted, never challenged the doctors. I could not accept it, any of it. I argued with her about the treatments, and about letting Paul off the hook, and what to do about the girls."

"You were trying to help. She understood that."

"She was right about all of it. About you too. But…." she pulled her hands free of the mug and shoved them into her lap as if she fought an urge to throw it or choke down the poison. "What I keep wondering is, how did she know?" She as swallowing tears, swiping at her cheeks, looking everywhere but at me. "And why didn't I?"

Still no hug when Mom went up to bed, but the hard place in my chest had loosened. Coffee mug in hand, I listened at the foot of the stairs to be sure they were all settled before I opened the kitchen door and followed the worn familiar path. Cool under my feet, the slate stones Dad and I had set years before carved a make-shift patio out of the overgrown grass, a Mother's Day surprise, no telling which year, but not long before he shot himself.

We would have to sell the house. I could not walk past the basement door every day and taste that failure over and over. And I could not sleep in my old bedroom. In a new place at least, I could stub my toes on a kitchen counter that was not where I expected it to be. Mom would have a new garden to organize. She might even come around and see it my way. Krissy would understand I could not handle the ghosts on top of everything else.

Sinking onto the rusted lawn chair, I let the cool air silt into my lungs. The kitchen light poured out a sloppy buttery blot on the disappearing yard—barely green fused into black nightshade. There, where the last fingernail of sunlight lapped at the edge of the bushes, the turquoise-tinged cobalt of hydrangeas framed a brighter circle.

Memory? Is that what tripped through those lengthening shadows, an awkward fatherless boy, and a girl so much smaller with her hand outstretched?

Wait for me. Tim, wait for me.

I stared into the backyard as it faded, the hydrangeas blots on the dark landscape. The voices, her voice, could have been across the hedge. Only once had she asked me about Dad. It had been the night before I went west, when I told her to ignore the rumors about Jade's baby, assured her it was not mine, that I wasn't running, just searching for something different.

"But you'll come back?" She meant not like our father. "And you'll call. I want to hear what you find out there. I want to hear about the world."

But she did not try to stop me. At thirteen, she knew better. I remember that night, how the stars shifted and disappeared behind blue-black clouds, how the streetlights striped the yard like prison bars. She hugged me goodnight and left me there, even though she knew I'd be gone in the morning. I wonder now, if she watched me from her bedroom window, if she cried, if she wished she'd tried to talk me into staying, if she felt abandoned, or if she fell asleep dreaming of the adventures I'd share when I returned, if she'd been sure I would be back.

There in the silent yard, in my funeral suit, I sat alone and wondered at the way life kept at you, poking and jabbing and calling your name. The past had been impossible to control. I had buried myself in made-up stories, in other people's journeys. I was struggling now to manage the present. Even as the shadows pressed closer, I sat up straighter. Maybe no one is ever alone. Maybe my father, unable to articulate what he was feeling, held us close until the bitter end. All during my wandering, without my realizing it, Krissy had kept the faith. My father might have felt that same faith. Not in himself, but in us. The only time I had felt that confident was when my nieces were in my arms.

Was it the past I was reaching for? My sister's hand in mine, her hugs, her face at the window, her voice reading out loud to her imaginary friends. Or was I reaching for some holograph of the future, an imagined summer evening years hence when I'd be calling *bedtime*, book in hand, chapter marked with a leftover mermaid napkin or a cereal box coupon, Krissy's almost smile, the whispery bedtime kisses of her girls—my girls now—and the promise of a new story from a different library.

I stood and stretched, noted the pale glow of a nightlight from the upstairs hallway outside their room. Leaving the shadows behind, I turned, climbed the back stoop, went inside, and turned off the backdoor light.

Love Me, Love Me Not by Norma E. Redfern
Riverside Chapter

I drank too much at dinner, unusual for me. I came home, jumped into the shower, hot water cascading down my back and clearing my head. I dried off and crawled naked between my satin sheets. After the hot shower, the cool touch of the sheets put me right to sleep. The phone rang. Who would call me at 3:45?

"Hello?" I heard Jonathon's voice and cringed. "What do you want? You do not understand. I want nothing more to do with you." I hung up the phone and fell back to sleep. The phone rang again. I looked at the clock: 4:23.

"Hello? Jonathon! What don't you understand? Don't call back."

Damn, would he ever learn? It was over. I had to be at work by eight. Getting up in two hours, I would be dragging.

The alarm went off, ringing in my head like a hammer hitting a metal wall. I rolled over and out of bed, staggered to the bathroom and splashed icy water on my face, hoping it would revive me. I dressed and headed out the door.

The store across the street had giant red hearts in the window, only three days until Valentine's Day. What a joke. I had broken up with Jonathan six weeks ago after I had caught him cheating for the second time.

Old romances and broken promises were the story of my life. Everywhere I went, hearts dangled in windows, roses for sale on every corner. I saw heart-shaped jewelry—all the secret ways to encourage love. Valentine's was a big money-making day. Fresh flowers and candy were delivered all over town. Lovers having candlelight dinners, music and wine. Naughty nighties and boxer shorts covered in hearts. Anything to make a buck, on the premise of the four-letter word: LOVE. I could not find any trust or integrity left in the world.

I stood on the corner of Oak and Main, waiting for the light. I was only a few blocks from the National Bank Building where I had been working for the past seven years. Thank God it was Friday.

A man standing opposite stepped off the curb to cross the street. A car barreled through the light and hit him, lipping his body like a rag doll into the air. He landed with a thud on the pavement. The car, a dark green BMW, slowed, and then sped away. I could not read the plates. I ran across the street to see if the man was still alive.

I reached his side. He lay still. He had been carrying a bouquet of yellow tulips, now scattered all around like petals at a wedding. A trickle of blood seeped from the corner of his mouth. I bent down and touched the side of his face. His skin felt warm and soft, with only a hint of a beard.

Sirens blared, and people shouted around me.

"Can you hear me?" I asked. To my relief, he opened his eyes. He had green eyes and dark curly hair with a little gray at the temples. I reached down and held his hand.

"Rebecca, where have you been? I was bringing you flowers," he said in a whisper, looking up at me. He sighed, reaching up to stroke my hair.

"We need to get through!" yelled the ambulance attendant, pushing his way into the crowd that formed around the two of us.

"Are you okay, Ma'am? Is this your husband?"

I straightened up and turned to see a police officer. "No, my name is Lee Ann Parrish. I saw the car run him down and tried to help." I did not realize tears streamed down my face. The officer took my arm and walked me to the patrol car.

"Can you tell me what happened?" he asked, taking

out a pad and pen. Answered several questions. Watched the injured man wheeled into the ambulance before I continued my way.

I was shaking when I arrived at work. Everyone wondered why I was late. After endless questions, I could finally get down to business. The morning went by quickly. I had little time to think about the stranger who carried a bouquet of tulips. After eating a quick lunch, I returned to the office. There on my desk sat a massive bouquet of daisies, with a large heart shaped card attached to the basket's side. Opening it up, I knew before I saw the name who it was from.

Jonathan, trying to win me back with flowers, could not even remember my favorites. I could have trashed them, but that would invite too many questions. I would leave them here. By Monday they would be dead, just like our three-year relationship. Toward the end of the day, I checked the news on my computer. The hit-and-run driver was still being sought. The victim was Wesley Marsh, his family had been notified. The article did not say much about his condition. I wondered why he called me Rebecca and touched my hair. I did not understand why I cried when I bent down and held his hand.

When I left work, instead of going home, I hailed a cab. "Take me to St. Luke's Hospital."

At the hospital, I asked for his room number. I took the elevator to the fifth floor. I approached the door as a man in a white coat came out.

"Are you Mrs. Marsh?" He looked at me. "I'm Mr. Marsh's doctor."

"No, I'm only a friend. Is he doing okay?"
"His condition is stable. Do not stay long. He needs to rest." He turned and left.

I went in. Mr. Marsh's head was wrapped in a turban of white gauze. The sheet was neatly folded across his chest as he lay flat on his back. His skin looked ashen, except for a bruise turning purple on the right side of his jaw. His beard had grown since this morning, now a dark shadow around his face. I stood by his side and touched his warm hand. He opened his eyes, blinking as he looked at me.

"Rebecca, where have you been? I was bringing you flowers." He spoke so softy I barely heard him.
I bent down, my hair falling, nearly brushing his arm. He reached up to caress the strands as he did this morning. Smiling at me, he clasped my hand. I said gently, "I'm not Rebecca, my name is Lee Ann."

He looked up at me and again reached for my hair. I saw tears glisten on his cheeks. Taking a tissue, I wiped each side of his face. He looked upset, maybe embarrassed by his crying.

"You're not Rebecca." He stared at me as though seeing me for the first time. He squeezed my hand. In a rasping voice, he told me about his wife Rebecca, who had died two years ago, on February 14th. He said how much he loved her, and he was taking her favorite flowers to the cemetery.

"That's sweet, you remembered what she liked." I had never met anyone who cared for me like that.

"What are your favorite flowers?" he asked.

Surprised by his question, I said, "Red carnations."

He tried to smile but winced in pain. "Your hair is the same color as Rebecca's, strawberry blonde, silky, long, and lovely."

I did not realize I still held his hand. He squeezed mine and a tingling sensation filled my body. My heart went out to him.

"Where's Rebecca buried?" I asked. I let go and pulled a chair to the side of the bed as he told me.

"Lee Ann, where are you from?" he asked, sounding tired.

"I'm from here, been here all my life. It is getting

late, and the doctor did not want me to stay a long time as you need to rest."

"Will you come back?"

"Yes, I'll be here tomorrow." I leaned over and kissed him on the cheek.

I got up early on Saturday morning. At the flower shop I bought a dozen yellow tulips, then grabbed a cab and went to Mount Olive Cemetery. I checked for the location of Rebecca Marsh's grave and the cabby drove there.

I returned to the hospital. Wesley, sitting up in bed, looked much better. I reached for his hand, "Rebecca's flowers have been delivered."

"Thank you, you don't know what that means to me. You are a kind and giving person. Any man who's in your life would be lucky." He smiled at me.

The door opened. I turned as a nurse brought in a bouquet of red carnations and handed them to me. My eyes filled with tears. Wesley had remembered my favorite flowers.

"Happy Valentine's Day. I want to take you to a special dinner when I am out of the hospital," Wesley said, gazing at me tenderly.

"You're a special man. I would be honored." I smiled at him, hoping this would be a new beginning for the both of us.

"The alarm went off, ringing in my head like a hammer hitting a metal wall."

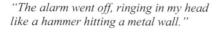

A Butcher Paper Almanac by Luke Wilson
Blue Ridge Writers

It gets quiet underground, late at night, within the guts of the city. Small sounds can grow inside this yawning throat of concrete, as they feed on the stale air. Sounds can hatch echoes down here, which sprout feet and wander about. At the moment, Matilda is half-asleep inside my coat. I wonder what shoes she thinks each noise would wear. A soft drip prattling into some dank corner would don baby clown shoes. Nearby, a lost breeze is caught in a stairwell where it pleads caution to the walls. It would wear sharp heeled stilettos and drag them over the pockmarked wooden floor. I sit listening beneath these whispers to a hum busy in its emptiness.

Nearly every night, I wait at Queen's Road Station and listen to the hum. I like it down here. As my memory dulls with age, I have come to find a certain comfort in familiar places. I always sit with Matilda at the same platform, on the same bench. Its wooden spine braces my vigil as I wait for that extraordinary hour, which comes every morning around half-past three.

At that time the platform becomes wholly deserted. Everything gets perfectly, doubtlessly still. Then I can focus my entire being on the hum. It consumes me, until by and by even the hum fades. Then I can hear beneath it— under the ordinary mantle of perception, past the dusty regolith, to a bedrock consciousness. This is when the trains start speaking to me. First, their metal hulls breathe and grumble like bellyaches. Then slowly, words come.

Their language is so faint and gentle that one must be empty of anything else before he can know it. It's more subtle than braille, owning a tacit sonorous geometry. Each word is shaped like an ornate rune, or hieroglyph. Each is a key that fits into any ear quiet enough to welcome it. Words glide in, one by one, turning over the brass tumblers and pins of a keyhole ear. Anyone can hear the trains. If only they were empty enough to listen.

I haven't slept in days, maybe a week. Matilda would know, but I don't want to rouse her. Her purring is so gentle now. Lately I have come to dread sleep, which only ever brings me the same nightmare. Besides, I can hear the trains better without rest. Too much dreaming waxes up my ears. Every night they say more to me, their voices are getting closer and clearer.

A slow herd of bodies is now drifting past my bench. Men crowned in wool caps and shod in heavy leather hooves. After they pass, I carefully take out my journal so as not to wake Matilda. I found the weathered suede book some time ago in the rubbish. The first couple of pages were filled with clumsy sketches of Westminster Abbey and Trafalgar Square. It must have belonged to a tourist. I kept the book and its ugly drawings.

I write in it every night once it's quiet enough to hear past the hum. I found a piece of charcoal too, which works well enough as a pen. With it, I transcribe everything the trains murmur. The weight of the book seems to grow as it collects these verses of trainsong. As I thumb through it, I can see that the early pages of my writing are testament only to strange letters and characters. Deeper in, these symbols gradually coalesce into words, then phrases. Half the journal is full of these curious, discordant lines. One passage reads:

perish bread / garden bone

Only the last marked page bears full sentences, but they are meaningless to me. The final words ask:

Is a bridge without a storm a foot caught between a puddle and grave?

I ease the journal back into my coat. I don't know what that last line means. I often forget the words, so I am forever pulling the book out again. It never does make much sense. Maybe tonight the trains will say more. Perhaps they will give me an answer to their last, or they may again leave me with riddles.

If not for Matilda, I would spend all my time down here. For her sake, I sometimes walk to the shelter at Fellows' Garden. It's north of the station across Blackfriars Bridge, in towards the heart of London. A few miles along busy cobblestone streets soiled with the horse-mud of carriages. I usually don't remember resolving to walk there, or much of the journey itself. Instead, I will simply discover myself again, in front of that old red door. The Salvation Army folks are nice enough. They don't like me wandering off and would love to fatten me up a bit. At Fellows' Garden, I get a good meal of scrag and bread that will last me a couple of days. And I wash Matilda. I bought her a fine Buffalo horn comb some time ago. That I do recall. I paid five shillings and begged half the winter to save enough. I remember that time fondly, even with the cold. Matilda's eyes lit up when she saw the comb. I keep the few pleasant memories I still have close to me, like firewood. They help sometimes.

I comb Matilda every day now, and she purrs so sweetly as I groom her. I coo-my-coos along to her melody. She is a tabby, with the gentlest face next to the moon, and a sweet custard smile. She's getting older, but I keep her chubby and clean. She sleeps in a sling I fashioned, which fits under my coat. Close enough to me that I can feel the air she breathes. Her little dream-hiccups and snores fill my clothes like warm incense. She smells as the wind might, if pulled through a bakery.

I close my eyes as I trace Matilda's scent. It draws me towards some hidden cistern of memory. For a moment, scenes appear flickering over the back of my eyelids. I see an attic full of children's toys. Then a kitchen with fresh lilac wallpaper. There is a woman in the kitchen with two small children. They look familiar, but I can't recall why. Just as the youngest child is turning towards me, I lose Matilda's fragrance. The kitchen fades with her scent, fast as dreaming. It doesn't trouble me so much. I am used to things disappearing. Briefly, under the blankets of leaden eyelids, I think I could sleep. But I know what horror my dreams hold, and I don't want to go back there.

When my eyes open, the woman and children are gone. There is only Matilda, asleep in my coat. She is always there, and I can't think of a time before her. She's not like other cats. I find her sometimes at Fellows' Garden, playing games with the spiders and mice she catches. She's always perfectly gentle and never hurts them. I wish I could afford her nicer things. Begging only allows me around twopence a day to buy her a bit of milk, and some lousy canned meat. She eats it like caviar all the same. She's been shedding a great deal lately and sleeps most of the time. But I try not to think about all that. I cannot fathom her getting sick.

My eyes settle on the wall across the tracks. It is spattered with advertisements for Viking Milk, Guinness, and Nestlé Chocolate. Among them are tan posters for the 1902 World's Fair shouting, *Wolverhampton Art and Industrial Exhibition!* Even if I wanted to go, I don't have the money for a ticket. Besides, I don't trust myself to travel that far alone. I can't honestly recall the last time I left London. It's better to stay here, close to the trains. Most of them are sleeping now. They rest like dark sieges of steel, dozing on cold gurneys over the obedient tracks. They look like the skeletons of once-great stallions— lumbering metal cadavers, with emaciated bodies starved down to ribs of rivets and welds.

The brass face of the platform clock says it's quarter-past three already. The last of the drunks are staggering slowly past me, in twos and threes. They are shrunk against the cold, but jubilant, high on the emancipation of darkness. They retreat into the city with the impetus of a dirty tide returning to a filthy sea. I shouldn't judge them, as I look just as worn and tattered. To a passerby, I would be yet another rough old man— once tall, perilously thin, wearing a pair of hazy rudderless eyes. But I'm not one of them. Only *I* am patient enough to hear the trainsong. And I believe there is a reason for that. I think the trains chose me, out of everyone at Queen's Road. I think they want to tell me something.

The platform is starting to empty, and I can hear the hum thicken. A pair of custodians in blue overalls sweep up nearby; they nod to me but say nothing. I think they have come to know me as yet another, particularly stubborn piece of trash. They sweep a wide berth around my bench, leaving such waste as myself for another, taller broom. I pat Matilda inside my coat. Just enough so she knows I am there, without waking her. I don't have time for the shame they expect of me. Soon it will be quiet enough.

The custodians' footsteps gradually recede, and I think Matilda would find their echo to wear soft downy slippers. It is finally time. I rise, quieter than a scar. First, I must wake the trains. Gingerly I move towards the dark flank of one sleeping iron stallion. The train is numbered *A45*, and red paint peels away from its cold metal skin. With one long index finger, I trace the stallion's raw jutting bones.

"Wake up, wake up, train. You have to wake up, wake up, train." I sing quietly, finger arguing with the soot, spinning slow circles. Looking up, I glimpse the face of an old man caught inside the glass of one train window. His coat is black, leaving a pale head to float bodiless in the dirty glass. His reflection appears sunken, greyed, ashen, collapsed under the weight of bones—eyes bible black, bloodshot, staggered for lack of sleep. He has the same silvery hair and tired eyes that I do.

Seeing this man reminds me of the faces in my nightmare. Except those faces are trapped in water, not glass. The dream is always the same. I stand beside a muddy river that flows inexorably towards a sheer waterfall. Dozens of bodiless faces writhe inside the river, fighting against the current. They swim paper-thin and frenzied, struggling to escape the falls. All of them strike me as familiar, although I can't match their likeness to any name. All the same, I think I knew them once. The river holds both children and elders. In the span of dreaming, there is only time enough to save one of them. The falls invariably take the others. It is to me to decide who lives, and the worst of it all is choosing. After my verdict, I race back and forth with cupped hands, carrying splashes of my chosen to a small hollow of ground. The more I fill it, the more the basin clouds with mud. In the last seconds before waking, the hollow is full. And the face I chose has a chance to clarify. Regardless of who I save, they always gasp bubbly sounds trying to declare themselves. In the moment of my waking, the basin collapses. Mud reclaims them. I never learn their names.

I move down the rails, away from that old man caught in the glass. I have no comfort to offer him. Maybe after I learn the trainsong, I can come back for him. Perhaps the newspaper will write about me. How out of everyone, only *I* was patient enough to hear the trains. Everyone would want to read about it, and I'd be rich enough to buy Matilda all the combs in the world. Even a whalebone one, inlaid with gold. Then, I could come back for that old man who looks like me, and the others in the river. I would like to know who they were to me.

Out of sight of the window, I let my finger dig a little moat in the grime. A small circle of pure, chaste-black metal appears, encroached on all sides by filth. I flatten out my whole palm, to clean a small island on the train's metal flank. "Someone should feed you more," I whisper to it. "Look after you, pat your coal belly. You look like a real carnivore to me. They should feed you some *meat*, some real *meat*, not rocks and oil."

I trace more circles and coo-my-coos, tangling through the heavy iron mane of soot and grease. The train stirs under my touch. I think they like it when I talk to them. I wish I could feed the train. I would feed it so tenderly, with a palm-full of smoked herrings, or Kippers, or whatever it wanted. I would feed it warm milk and honey, like Matilda.

Beneath my hand, I can feel the train begin to wake. The hum ripens with it. With my clean hand, I pat Matilda inside my coat. Then, I focus all of myself on the hum. As it grows, every other pocket of my awareness recedes, as if fleeing from a tall seismic wind. In the space left behind, the hum consummates into trainsong. Letters appear, slowly at first. They gradually meld together into the cursive latticework forms of words. They begin to arrive quicker, faster than ever before, in a torrent of language. Before I have time to reach for my journal, the first words come. The train sounds ancient and creaking:

> *"Welcome, Wes."* The train says. *"Don't worry too much about today; tomorrow will be another. Another butcher paper almanac, another pound of bacon scrap porridge, all gristle and silverskin poached over easy; you'll have to baby the eggs, baby the eggs, yolks are such fragile creatures. They break when we say too much about nothing. Truth also has a fragile yolk; it must be poached in just enough nothing, so as to please it. Not a little too less. You are different, Wes. You are the first one quiet enough to hear me. You should find a Truth, something Eternal, something Real. And*

*write it all out so ugly it cannot help but stay real.
Then everyone will listen."*

I stumble back from the train, a thin island inside my vast black coat. Never before has one said so much to me, or so quickly. Usually they take minutes to begin, slowly chewing on their first vowels. Even as I stand, the train is still singing out. These words feel too great for the pages of my journal. I need to find a better canvas.

I limp hastily toward a trash bin, right across from a red-on-white advertisement for Viking Milk. "You can't write much of a manifesto on milk and biscuits, can you?" I mumble excitedly, digging through the rubbish. Matilda stirs, and I pat my coat. "I'm sure you could Matilda, you'd write Shakespeare on nothing but hominy and cantaloupe. But the rest of us aren't so lucky."

Newspapers, stale wrappers, crumpled damp scraps. Somewhere in the mess, I find a large, reasonably clean, piece of brown wrapper paper. Wasting no time, I move back to my bench. Once I smooth the paper across my lap and gather my charcoal, everything is finally ready. This creamy alabaster parchment in my hands becomes sacrosanct, inviolable, pure as newborn baby toes. It is waiting to carry my message.

I write as fast as I can without smearing the clumsy rod of charcoal. It struggles to mark the waxy paper, whose brown skin knuckles and creases. The page dances like a bronco buried in thin dirt. Blazed, lit on paper wings, my words are freed from deeper stables. Fielded again, they graze in open pastures across this page. Matilda fusses within my coat like she can smell the intensity.

The faster and deeper I write, the louder the train moans. It builds into a frenzied head of steam. Nearby the other trains start to wake and lend their voices in harmony as a fugue, which blends tumult towards a pounding crescendo. This bedlam wail presses me on, into a purer urgency, to speak their words through me. The pitch of their storm only builds, begging for that cadence of release—iron walls of sound press close against my body, crushing it, cresting mercilessly, rising in a thick and wrathful eyewall, like some cyclone tied my body across its sheer precipice. My only salvation is to complete their message before I am crushed beneath the weight of it.

Matilda startles and springs out the top of my coat, but she can't be out in this storm alone! It will trample her little bones! No matter how much milk I feed her, it will never be enough for her bones to stand under this weight. Matilda streaks away across the platform. She runs heavily, her coat patchy from all the shedding. She hides inside a nearby shadow and waits for me to comfort her. She spins around in circles, looking back toward me at the crux of each rotation—as she always does when she wants to be picked up. I would reach out to her, but I am so nearly done. There is no longer space in my lungs to hold back this storm, so I shout into its onslaught, "Matilda! It's ok. Soon everybody will know!"

The charcoal floats words for trainsong, filling brown butcher paper. From some ways off a new sound is building, hurtling down the rails toward us. Matilda coils away from this threat, pressing her taut fear into the wall. She seems so taken with fright that she could dart away. I would go now and comfort her, but I have never been this close before to grasping the essence of trainsong.

I finally understand. I am a prophet to these trains, and they will use my voice to be known. I write facing Matilda, witness to her providence, her grace, her Godliness. She would understand that destiny doesn't wait; understand this is my time, which will never come again. When all of this is through, and everyone has heard my trainsong, we will both be rich—and I will buy her all the finest sardines and sweetmeats, and she will sleep on a goose down pillow, and we will live in a big empty house, where she can play her gentle games all day with the mice and spiders. And there will be a train station in the basement where we will sit at night and hear the trains coo-their-coos and sing. And I will save all those faces who look like me from the river. And finally, I will be able to rest. And sleep in empty white linen dreams.

A Murder of Crows by Rick Hodges
Northern Virginia Chapter

It was 1954, and everyone was scared of communists under their beds, so I took it in stride when the motel manager told me about the murder in the room.

"It's the only room left," she said, her cigarette swaying between her lips as she spoke, "if you're okay with it. We changed the sheets."

I was young then and didn't creep out easily. Also, it was the last room and the next motel was 15 miles down the road.

After I signed the register, the manager offered some more information I did not ask for.

"It might not have been a murder—they didn't find a body in the room, just blood. The man was gone, but his luggage and car were still here. The police searched everywhere."

As long as there's no dead body in the room, I mused, I will be happy.

The room was fine. No signs of blood that I could see. No eerie feeling; no shiver in my spine. A decent room with a color TV. I had a two-week stay ahead of me to do a training gig for my employer—I trained insurance agents, town-to-town. I'd been on the road a while and slept like a baby. No ghosts or nightmares disturbed my slumber.

But I did get an early start.

The crows woke me before sunrise. They cawed and screeched outside my window. When the sun rose, I laughed—about a dozen of the noisy black birds were perched on a scarecrow on the plot of farmland across the road. A scarecrow that wasn't scaring crows. The scarecrow looked forlorn, as if asking for help to repel the birds. His body sagged, straining the wooden cross he was tied to. His head was a burlap sack with holes cut out for eyes. Someone had put real-looking eyes in its eye sockets, and they were staring at me through the window. Even the eyes did not frighten these crows, though. What a sad-sack scarecrow.

On the way out to the local insurance office, I gave the poor scarecrow a helping hand and shooed the crows off with a threatening wave of my arms. "Get away!" Stupid crows! "You woke me up before the alarm clock." Most of them flew off, cawing their disapproval at me.

After a day of training, I stopped for a sandwich at the tiny diner attached to the motel. "You the one in that room?" said a rugged-faced man drinking coffee. I told him yes—we both knew what room he meant.

"You ain't scared?"

"No. Things like that don't bother me."

"They ain't found the body. The sheriff searched all over. Nothing." He took a sip of coffee. "They dug all around the motel. Poked around my land, too." He motioned with the coffee cup at the field across the road. So he was the farmer with the incompetent scarecrow.

"Did they catch the killer, though?" I asked.

"The paper said the state police pulled over someone with a plate that matched to a guest here at the motel, 'bout a hundred miles west, but there wasn't nothing in his car and they had to let him go."

"Did they look in the trunk?"

"Course they looked in the trunk. No sign of a dead body, no blood, not nothing. He musta hid the body somewhere 'round here. The sheriff's deputies searched all over but couldn't find nothing."

I was tired from the rude wake-up call and long day, so I left for my room. "Your scarecrow is having some trouble scaring crows," I told the farmer on the way out.

"Yeah, crows are funny that way," he said, "but there ain't no crops up this time of year for them to get into so it don't matter none."

So the crows weren't there to raid Old Man

Farmer's vegetables, they were just there to annoy me.

They did a good job of it. I awoke to the cawing before sunup again. This time I had closed the curtains, but it was not enough to stop the damn noise. When the sunlight peeked through the curtains and I opened them, I saw that even more birds had gathered to taunt the useless scarecrow, and some were pecking at his head. His eyes looked at me even more pathetic, as if begging for some assistance.

If the scarecrow could not do its job, I could at least get revenge. On my way to my car, I grabbed an empty Coca-Cola bottle. I hurled it at the crows. But my throw fell way short, and the glass broke on the edge of the road. A few crows startled, but none flew off.

I spent another bleary-eyed day teaching insurance agents how to fill out forms and mail carbon copies to the central office. When I got back to the motel, even more crows were gathered, pecking, and tearing at the pathetic scarecrow. His eyes seemed to follow me, begging for relief, as I went in my room and hit the bed.

As I said before, when I arrived at the motel, I was not the type to scare easily. But that changed.

In a deep sleep, I dreamed that I heard a man moaning in pain and desperation. I could not see him because I had some kind of cloth over my head. Then the voice cried, "Help me," but I could hear that he knew he was beyond help and death was certain soon. Then I dreamed that I removed the cloth from my head and saw him standing at the door of my motel room. He stared at me, his eyes bright in the dark room. His blood was pulsing from gashes in his chest as his heartbeat for the last time. From his eyes, I knew that he had reached that point where death was certain, and he could do nothing with his last moments but wait for his last heartbeat to come. As terror overcame me, I sensed he was dead, but he did not fall to the floor. His blood drained into the carpet, and I dreamed the blood was climbing up the bed toward me. I froze in fear until the terror woke me.

I lay there for several minutes, catching my breath and rejoining reality as my body shook. It was still dark, but the moon shone through the crack in the curtains.

Then I heard the crows again.

I was still tense from the nightmare. I did not wait for the sun to rise this time. I threw on a bathrobe, and with only the moon to guide me, I strode across the road to the gathering of noisy crows perched on the useless scarecrow.

I had no plan beyond shooing the birds again, but then I realized I could knock the whole scarecrow down and fix them for good. In the dim light, I could see the scarecrow's white eyes fixed on me as I approached. The crows cawed louder as they sensed me coming near, but they seemed to laugh at me.

I got close enough to look the scarecrow in the eyes. But one eye was missing.

Suddenly the black birds all took to the air, several brushing me with beaks and claws. I raised my arms in my defense and stumbled backward, falling to the earth. A single crow landed on the ground in front of me. It held something in its beak that it dropped before flying off into the dark.

A human eyeball lay on the ground, staring at me.

Touching on the Past by Judy Whitehall Witt
Richmond Chapter

Franklin grabbed the listing stack of old photo albums. The top one slid off, landing on the floor with a slap. A cloud of dust bloomed from the cover.

"Do you have anyone in the family who'd want to take these albums, Ray?" asked Franklin. He'd been hired to help Ray downsize and move into assisted living.

Ray picked up the one on the floor and ran his gnarled fingers over the tattered cover, gently stroking the embossed roses. "I'll be taking them with me."

Franklin's brows pinched in puzzlement. The hodgepodge of fifteen unique albums would never set easily on a shelf, if there was a spare one to be had. Ray's tight new quarters allowed only for the barest essentials. "But…"

"These hold my memories in place. When you get to my age, it's about all you've got. Here, let me show you." Ray laid the album on the coffee table and opened it.

Franklin watched Ray put his finger on one faded photo that had come loose from the first page and lodged in the binding.

"Ah, yes. This is one of my favorites. It shows four generations of us. I'm the baby in my mother's arms. Wasn't she a looker? And there's Grandma and Oma, my great-grandmother."

Ray gingerly turned two pages and slid his index finger to the nearly ruined photo in the lower right corner. A crease cut diagonally across the fuzzy profile of a droopy-eared mutt. "Now here was my best friend, Nibs. Come hell or high water, that dog would never leave my side. He was trampled to death by a horse just days after this was taken." Tears dribbled from Ray's unfocused eyes.

The squeak of crepe-soled shoes on hardwood announced the arrival of Ray's private nurse, Marjory.

"Is it that time already?" Ray asked. "We were just getting to the good stuff."

"Your appointment is at two. We need to get going if we're to be on time," Marjory replied.

Ray stood and, with the erect bearing only an old soldier can muster, marched to his front door. "Franklin, mind you put those albums in the carton carefully. Don't let any of the loose photos slide out of place."

"Yes, sir."

Of all the... Franklin could not believe what he was seeing.

Ray had taken a white-tipped cane from the umbrella stand and tap-tapped his way out to the waiting car.

Jesus Saves Church by David Barudin
Valley Chapter

The rain came down harder and colder in a precursor of the winter snowstorms that would soon blanket Des Moines and Iowa and the entire Midwest until the spring rains released them. In the streetlights, slanting stilettos of sleet stung my face. No matter. I kept walking. No destination. Just the end of the block and make a turn. My apartment was too many street corners back to be sure how far or which way I'd come.

Neither could I say exactly how I came to be in my current circumstances, or where this slide began. I left my job less than a year after college. It was 1970 and many in the country's largest generation, the Early Baby Boomers like me born on the heels of WWII, were uprooting to travel and *find themselves*. The Hippies in the Sixties called it *dropping out*. The Yuppies came up with *copping out*. In retrospect, they were all dubious pursuits by relatively few who were looking to put off conventional careers like those of our parents.

I first read about VISTA in Battery Park where I took lunch breaks from my windowless cubicle in the financial district of Lower Manhattan. The *New York Times* called VISTA the domestic Peace Corp and a vanguard in LBJ's War on Poverty. I wasn't insensitive to the plight of the poor. I had marched in college, but that was mainly for the pot and girls. Pure and simple, VISTA was a convenient and respectable lifeboat cushioned with a living stipend and I was jumping ship.

For reasons I'll explain, I was kicked out before my volunteer year was up. My girlfriend, also a VISTA, split up with me on account of it. Suddenly, I was a casualty of both love and LBJ's war, stranded in storm-battered Iowa with winter coming on and rent due, taking to stalking the streets of not the safest of neighborhoods.

Rounding a corner, a frigid gust of wet wind caught me head on and pushed me into the rippling tide coursing down the street. A loud thunderclap spun me around. A lightening flash revealed a dimly lighted patch in the dark sodden sky. I could barely make out the blurred neon *Jesus Saves* in the interstices of a cross. I headed toward it, splashing through the reflection of a stained-glass window splattered on the saturated street like a smashed Christmas tree.

Underneath the church overhang, I pressed an ear to the heavy wood door. It held the muffled voices of a revival hymn. I hesitated to go in. I was not a member. I was not even Christian, or from Iowa. My closest connection to Jesus and the state was my ex-girlfriend, a non-observant "jack" Mormon from southern Utah whose VISTA assignment was in Iowa, like mine had been. Thinking about her now, I could not have imagined the unseen forces that drew us together would also conspire to deposit this miserable, soaked cast-off outside the Jesus Saves Church.

When I first saw her at VISTA training less than a year before, she was stepping from a cab, a tall girl in a tight, knee length orange skirt-suit. One hand billed her forehead from the sun that caught her blond hair and turned it the color of white gold. Her other hand pulled a yellow valise like a squared-off golden retriever on a leash. I was helping register the new arrivals and shot straight over to her and reached for the strap, a gesture she mistook for a handshake and the valise dropped with a thud. She had a strong grip when we shook. I was glad that I was a little taller than her.

"And you are?" I asked her in an official tone, holding a clipboard prominently in front of me. Her voice came in a clear, bright shape that matched her face and blue eyes that had little green flecks in them. I repeated her name back to her. "Oh, yes, here you are."

Falling in love had not been a choice. Instead, a few moments and the right timing meant everything. As it turned out, I discovered that escaping New York to *find myself* was about finding someone else. Someone whose eyes reflected my best self and held in them a world of potential and possibilities. Falling in love, to me, meant validation of my not just accepting what life put in front of me after college. In an instant, this leapt out at me from blue eyes with dancing green specks like tiny universes.

I slouched against the Jesus Saves door.

"You jist gonna stand out here in the rain or you comin' in?" Said a figure in a hooded rain slicker brushing past me into the church.

I followed her into the brightly lit vestibule and watched her descend steps where warm cooking smells rose and engulfed me. For a few minutes I simply stood inside the door, the linoleum pooling under me. The gold and purple robed choir overflowed the altar like a flowering vine. Some of the singers faced each other and others extended their arms to the half-filled hall. None held hymnals. The mostly Black congregation stood swaying in unison. The worn hardwood floor creaked under them. Halos of light from sconces between the stained-glass windows looped the honey-colored plaster walls up to the vaulted ceiling. No one seemed to notice me standing in a small pond in the foyer or heard my teeth chattering or felt the chill that poured off me.

I climbed the stairs to the balcony and found a seat at the front railing. The young Black preacher in a dark tailored suit addressed the congregation in a commanding baritone voice.

"Amen. Jesus is with us tonight."

The choir dropped to a hum and a billowing response of *Amen* and *Yes Jesus* echoed from the assemblage. The preacher leaned out from the pulpit, angling his chin up toward the balcony. Some of the faces below me followed his gaze. I shrank down in the pew, feeling conspicuously wet and not Black. I glanced around for the quickest way out but thought better of bringing added attention to myself. Anyway, what was there to run from? And where would I go? I shrank farther back in my seat.

The preacher raised a hand to the balcony and his voice rang out, "There are those among us here with Jesus tonight who are down on their luck. Who are hurting. In pain. Who are broken."

A swell of "Amen" and "Yes Jesus" rose up from below and from around me in the gallery. The choir sang a chorus of "Bringing in the sheaves. Waiting for the harvest, and the time of reaping. We shall come rejoicing, bringing in the sheaves." The minister shouted above them, "Jesus sees you. Jesus knows everything about you and your trials." He was looking at me. Another rush of *Amen*s and *Yes Jesus*es with a few discernable *Dear Jesus*es welled up through the boards under my feet. Then he said, "All who are pained raise your hands; raise your hands to Jesus. That's right; get 'em up."

Before I fully realized what I was doing, my hand was in the air.

The preacher cried, "Come down here in front of the altar and lay down your troubles. Jesus is here to pick them up. If you believe, come down. If you believe just a little, come down. If you don't know and are confused, come down. Jesus is here for you tonight, brothers and sisters."

I must have made a movement to stand because several people close by sprang to help me down the narrow stairs and out among the half-dozen downtrodden souls who were shuffling to the altar. I looked for a side door but the preacher rushed to grip my shoulders. He asked me if I believed Jesus was my Lord and Savior?

I felt the weight that had momentarily lifted with his hands on my shoulders suddenly return. "That's a problem," I whispered.

He jerked his head back and looked at me, and then he slowly smiled and nodded. He lifted his gaze to the congregation. "Glory be to God! We have one of the Chosen People among us tonight."

You could hear a pin drop in the Jesus Saves Church. Without pausing, he went on for several minutes about the Israelites and Black folk in America, both long-suffering peoples risen from bondage to wander in deserts of despair and torment. *Amen* and *Yes Jesus* came from all over the hall. The preacher was not about to let me off the hook, even if I wasn't Christian. He turned his dark liquid stare back fully on me.

He said, "Son, It doesn't matter what you think may have brought you here tonight. I know who brought you here. However heavy your load is, He will take it up. However burdensome, He will carry it. Will you give it to Him?" He tightened his grip on my shoulders, reassuringly. When I didn't respond right away, he added, "Do you believe He can do that for you, son?"

At that point I was ready to give anyone, anything, credit that could even come close. I had quit a prosperous future career to become a volunteer in a vague search for who I was. And the answer, as it turned out, was not who I hoped for. Maybe Jesus was more than the son of a poor Jewish contractor. Who was I to say? At least I could pledge that I would never say he was not. I must have given the preacher that impression because he smiled and retreated to the altar in a chorus of *Amen Jesus*es.

After the storm and the Jesus Saves Church, I began piecing together how to extricate myself from the pit I was in. If my ex-girlfriend had taught me anything it was the value of change, even just for the sake of it, and the fruitlessness of blame and regret and other negatives. She did hatha yoga every day and practiced meditation. She took supplements and did not eat meat. Other VISTA's called her Nature Girl.

So, I embraced my misery and loss. All the feelings of abandonment. Even regrets and extreme loneliness. These were primal emotions, in her words, no different than love. Primal emotions either were, or they were not. You did not kind of fall in love or were a little miserable. Accordingly, I had to acknowledge and face them in the moment, as part of *finding myself* and getting my girlfriend back.

Also, there really was not another option. It was what the cards had dealt me. I still walked all hours of the day and night. I scrounged up the next month's rent waiting tables at Hojo's (which also saved on groceries) and took other part-time jobs. I returned to Jesus Saves Church a few times to talk with Reverend Mike, who was a sympathetic and scholarly confidant.

I slept sporadically, dreading the first gray light creeping in the window of my apartment and across the face looking back at me in the bathroom mirror when I got up. But I got up, washed, shaved, and had breakfast. I scripted a plan for when I'd feel confident enough to confront my ex-girlfriend and tell her what I didn't tell her and other VISTA's when I left the program. She still was not answering my calls or letters. So, my scripted plan had to account for any scenario I'd encounter. Still, I hesitated pulling the trigger.

As it turned out, how it all came down was beyond anything I could've scripted.

Facing winter on the Great Plains, VISTA volunteers on assignments stretching from Cedar Rapids, Iowa, to North Platte, Nebraska, were ready to party. My departure provided the excuse for our class of trainees to gather in Des Moines. They rolled in for the weekend and crashed at VISTA pads wherever the night's revelry deposited them. My ex-girlfriend was conspicuously absent.

On Sunday all the partygoers converged on the farmhouse in Jasper County, thirty miles from Des Moines, that my ex shared with three VISTA ladies. It was a perfect party house, large and secluded. The caravan of cars snaked up the county two-lane a mile from the state road and parked in the barren cornfields harvested a month earlier surrounding the tall white house. I looked around the place, checked the barn and sheds, but her 350cc Honda motorcycle she had shipped from home wasn't there.

The VISTA supervisor made an obligatory appearance. I liked him and regretted the situation that precipitated his firing me. What he said when he had called me down to his office a month earlier still rang in my ears: "Shit, Walker, I gotta let you go."

I pointed out I had violated VISTA's policy that volunteers work behind the scenes in their assigned communities, keeping a low profile, avoiding publicity, or drawing attention to themselves. Instead, I had become a familiar face at City Hall. With my business degree and work experience, writing federal matching grants to fund councilmen's pet improvement projects, called Model Cities in Johnson's Great Society, was a snap. But Nixon was cutting back poverty programs and trying to shut down VISTA and the OEO. Money for lighted basketball courts and a reconditioned neighborhood center made good local news in Des Moines. But the timing was bad. The VISTA supervisor had gotten an earful after I was interviewed on the nightly news and was pictured with the mayor in *The Des Moines Register & Tribune*.

The VISTA supervisor appealed to me to resign. The newspaper would have a field day if he fired me, he said. More unwanted publicity. He briefly held out the possibility of an administrative job with the agency in another city. When I asked him how much it paid, he tapped his pencil on the government surplus metal desk and glared at me. The message was clear. There was no job. I was out. And that was that. He was under fire and I kept my mouth shut to other VISTA's. My story held. I'd officially resigned.

Shortly after the announcement, my girlfriend showed up at my apartment. She stormed past me and the rest of my world toppled in.

"You quit? We just heard it at the meeting today. You obviously weren't there. When were you going to tell me?" She shouted over me. "Why didn't you talk to me first?"

I started to explain and stammered, started over.

She said, "This affects my life, too, you know. I thought we had an understanding. Well, I guess I misunderstood."

I reminded her how she embraced change as being a good thing, the single constant in life, and that it always turned out for the best. Her view of change and mine on *finding yourself* were not that different. They were something a Utah farm girl and a Jersey boy had had in common. I said, "I thought you'd—"

She stopped me with a steely look and walked to the door. Her voice rose plaintively. "That's just it. It's not just you quitting and not telling me. But you assume you know how I feel. You don't. I wonder if you ever did."

"I was going to tell you," I said as she pushed past me out the door.

She hopped on the Honda and gunned it. "When were you going to tell me? When you figured out how to persuade me it was for us? For me? Like you think you know what's best for me? I hate that. It's why I left Utah."

As she pulled away, she shouted not to follow her or call the farmhouse. But I left long unanswered messages, anyway. Then, the party weekend happened.

On Sunday of the party weekend, I went in the farm house the girls rented and her three roomies ushered me upstairs into a parlor room off the landing and shut the door. VISTA's came from all occupations and backgrounds and were of all ages. You got to know their circumstances well. They were glad to share. The required sensitivity sessions at VISTA training were looked forward to everyone.

The three roommates were no exceptions. Tall bespectacled Mary Plotkin, a former Connecticut elementary school teacher, poked my chest with a long purple painted fingernail. In her other hand was a keg-shaped bottle of Red Stripe beer. Not normally a drinker, Mary was already past her two-beer limit.

"Sheesh too good for you, you know, and you're a shelfish—" she stammered. Her angular frame leaned precipitously and her long brown hair hung across one side of her face.

I stared at her. "I'm a shellfish, Mary?"

"A shelfish bashtard."

The other two women lowered her into an armchair. Mert Blinn was from Ohio. She was short and compact

with eyes swimming in thick glasses, like blue pufferfish magnified against the side of their bowls. Mert pried Mary's beer out of her hand.

"I really have to talk to her," I said, my gaze still on Mary.

She shook her head. "Noshir, my lipsh are shield. Butcha know what, you a good guy and I love you bofe."

Standing on the other side of Mary was Patsy O'Meara, from South Boston, previously a BU undergrad who had spent most of her college time in the pubs along Commonwealth Avenue before joining up. Patsy gave me a resigned smile. "Kyla's not letting many people in right now, Walker. Can you blame her?"

"Sheesh heartbroken," said Mary, despondently.

Heartbroken. I could've kissed Mary for saying that. Instead, a *thank you Jesus* under my breath drew surprised looks. I told them about the Jesus Saves Church. "I promised the preacher I'd make a donation if I got her back," I said.

"How much?" Mert asked.

I had not thought about it. "Generous," I said.

The two girls standing next to the armchair exchanged looks over Mary's head and took long pulls on their Red Stripes. Patsy downed hers and took Mary's from Mert and finished it off.

"You didn't quit VISTA, did you?" Patsy asked.

When I had finished telling them the whole story, Mert, Patsy, and Mary were the only VISTA's who knew about my nondisclosure agreement with the VISTA office. When I confirmed that the agency and OEO were facing cuts and both could be dismantled, all three shook their heads. They had figured it but did not know for sure, they said.

We had a group hug, another propensity of VISTA's. Too bad it had come down on me, they commiserated, and said they would've done the same thing if they were in my shoes. I told them they would've known better than to be in my shoes.

Downstairs, the party was in full swing. More VISTA's and the county Head Start office arrived along with a few off-duty county deputies with wives or girlfriends and six-packs in hand. An unseasonably warm night for late fall, the sky was filling with stars and a new moon rose above the trees that bordered the vacant fields. The air was redolent with the smells of turned earth, cows, and whole pot plants in black trash bags that people smoked in large water bongs or rolled into fat joints. The deputies blithely turned a blind eye. Jethro Tull, Jefferson Airplane, and the mile-a-minute licks of Alvin Lee and Ten Years After blared on the turntable.

In the kitchen, a volunteer we called Haystack for his thatch of blond hair trimmed off his shoulders like mounded straw, poured cooking oil and dried peas into a big iron frying pan. Smoking a joint the size of a cigar, he turned the burner on high and set the iron lid in place. Stoned as he was, he managed to vigorously shake the heavy skillet without dropping it. The loud popping drew a crowd into the kitchen. To everyone's amazement, perfectly formed green popcorn lifted the lid and overflowed the counter.

In the ensuing moment of spontaneous astonishment, laughter erupted in the farmhouse kitchen mosh pit and Kyla bumped against me and took my hand. Not a word was said that might ground the electric connection that flowed through our hands. We fell into her bed almost immediately.

I woke in the middle of the night from a nightmare that I was back in my apartment having to face the morning mirror and another empty day. It took a few minutes to register that it was a dream and that Kyla was nuzzled in the crook of my shoulder.

A Way to a Gobber's Heart by John L. Dutton, II
Write by the Rails

*How do you stop an alien invasion? Why everyone knows
that the way to a man's heart is through his stomach, and
that goes the same for aliens!*

Earth, May 12, 2055

My name is Walter, Walter Retlaw, but my friends call me
Wally. Now, what happened today started way back, so
before I can go on and tell you about today, I have to get
you up to speed with some background knowledge.

In 1998, some guys with big brains at the
Massachusetts Institute of Technology, otherwise known as
MIT, developed the Transiting Exoplanet Survey Satellite
[TESS] to survey the brightest stars near the Earth for
transiting exoplanets, planets outside our solar system, over
a two-year period. As it just so happened, TESS detected
planet GJ 357 b, a "hot earth" that orbits much closer to its
parent star which allows the planet to sustain human life.
You might think the United States of America would
launch a space probe to go check such an important
discovery out. You know, like the New Horizons space
probe sent to do a flyby study of Pluto in 2006. New
Horizons completed their mission, but it took ten years to
reach Pluto. Ten years! Let that sink in, and Pluto is *inside*
our solar system. Now you get to the heart of the problem:
This "hot earth" was 31 light-years from our Solar System,
so no one thought much about GJ 357 b given that it would
take around 260,000 years to get there. Nothing happened
for quite a while until July 2019, when TESS detected a
"Super Earth" within the circumstellar habitable zone. This

is a zone that was determined to be an area that could sustain human life. Then, just like that, BAM! The race to planet GJ 357 b was open full throttle!

Before long, everyone wanted in on the act. It was the Space Race of the 1960s all over again, and Russia was not holding back. No way was the United States going to play second fiddle to anyone, so in August 2019, President Donald Trump formed the U.S. Space Force.

"Space Com will defend America's vital interest in space, the next war-fighting domain," President Trump told reporters in August 2019.

Now let's forget about the chest poundings and all the bravado between those two great nations, because both Russia and the U.S.A. never came close to claiming planet GJ 357 b. The fools forgot a basic rule: *If I can see you, then you can see me.* That is exactly what happened. Earth was invaded in March 2022 by the inhabitants of planet GJ 357 b. NASA's finest determined that the invaders, now known as G'Jobbers, used our own satellite feed to track a route that led them straight to Earth. To their advantage, their technology can travel 31 light-years in approximately three years.

When the G'Jobbers massive starship warped into our atmosphere, mass hysteria ensued. However, the mammoth starship just sat outside our atmosphere for months systematically scanning the planet as if Earth was a patient taking an MRI scan. If you have ever had one, the G'Jobbers' scan sounded like the annoying thumping when inside that damn machine.

Nothing on our planet could penetrate the starship's defenses. Along with the "Rooskies," Trump's vaulted U.S. Space Force proved impotent. The G'Jobbers not once offered a counterattack. They just kept scanning the planet. According to our world leaders, the G'Jobbers were studying us.

To avoid any potential hostilities, President Donald Trump invoked Marshall Law and appointed himself Commander and Chief. The race to befriend the G'Jobbers was on.

On his Twitter feed, President Trump tweeted, "Pucker up, Rooskies! We're about to kiss some G'Jobber ass – and no one kisses ass better than the U.S. of A."

The G'Jobbers were studying us, and eventually made contact. They were a friendly race, and every opportunity and accordance were made to keep them that way.

And now, there we are, and here I am.

The best way to kiss ass is by wining and dining your opponent as you try to pull the wool over their eyes. This is where I fit into this story. I am here because Trump appointed me the personal chef of the G'Jobber leader, whose name is so unpronounceable, that I just called it, Gobber. My appointment was an easy decision for Trump to make seeing how I was his personal chef's young apprentice. "The Donald" was never going to appoint the G'Jobbers *HIS* personal chef.

Trump's tweet: "Because we know a way to a man's heart is through his stomach, I am sending my most talented personal chef to the G'Jobbers' leader. My taste buds will miss him, but this is a sacrifice I am willing to make to keep the peace."

What a crock of shit. I graduated from a community college culinary school with an associate degree. The only reason I was hired in the first place was because I was used as leverage in a blackmail scheme on the part of my mother. Ten years ago, when she was Managing Director for Trump International Hotel in Washington D.C., she had of a torrid affair with our illustrious Commander and Chief. Regardless of how I got the appointment, I was happy to have the job because, I will admit it, I love to cook.

So, there I was, twenty years old and straight out of culinary school. I was wide-eyed and bushy tailed. However, I did not stay that way. I learned the ins and outs of being a personal chef through baptism by fire, but I've learned much more from being so close to Gobber. I watched, I studied, and I learned things on the inside. Things no one else knows.

That's how my life has played out. For thirty-three years I have had, for the most part, the pleasure of preparing the food for Gobber and Gobber's Chiefs of Staff. I've heard the expression, "It's lonely at the top," but I witness loneliness firsthand. Often times, Gobber dines alone, and

I'm Gobber's sole companion. After serving the evening meal, Gobber invites me to stay. I do not want, need, or demand anything, and Gobber likes that. We just talk, or as Gobber would say, "Ohhhok okak gagrr."

In those thirty-three years, I have learned the G'J's language, offered untold hours of advice, and tried to make their transition to Earth as smooth as possible. Oh, and I have also learned Gobber's favorite meals.

During our time together, I learn to forgive Gobber's vulgar eating habits and to keep my hands and fingers away from Gobber's piranha like teeth. Though I have tried countless times to refine Gobber's grace and charm, I fight a losing battle. Because of my steadfast devotion, Gobber treats me as an equal, which always amazes me. We are far from equal. Gobber stands almost nine feet tall and I am only 5'6". Gobber walks like Shaggy from the old Scooby Doo cartoons, except being more bowlegged. My size elevens are no match for Gobber's size twenty-two feet. I cannot believe how many times Gobber has stepped on me. Oh, it's easy to do with feet shaped like a lady's high heel shoe that spreads out into scuba fin instead of a point. By putting up with all of this, I have earned Gobber's trust. Years ago, Gobber sent away the official tasters and now enjoys the delicacies I prepare without question.

Often, Gobber joins me in the ship's galley and watches me prepare the evening meal. During these times, Gobber confides in me. All that scanning and studying really has not helped Gobber's race garner anything substantial. Gobber wants to learn the ways of our world, and I mean everything. Gobber wants to know how, even with eight stomachs, a bulbous body that shakes like jelly, a lingering putrid stench, and a "face" of a rotting corpse, just how "to walk and talk like a lady." Yes, I am living the 21st century version of *My Fair Lady,* or, as I like to call it, *My Fair G'Jobber*. Gobber wants to learn everything I know. So, I become Gobber's Rosetta Stone and then some. At the same time, Gobber's teaching me, except Gobber does not even know it. Gobber's language comes out of the back of my throat, and I sound like I'm constantly gargling mouthwash.

I place video cameras throughout the starship and instill upon Gobber the need to practice proper English and rules of etiquette at all times. I prepare phrases on flashcards for Gobber to practice. The two that are always in need of constant practice are: "Walter is a true friend" [Ahhk grrck haaaa eck] and "Do not question me again." [Arrgh kaa kawwak taka]. We watch the videos during the evening meal, and I offer pointers and Gobber peppers me with questions. Thirty-three years later, Gobber still has not garnered any pertinent knowledge of the ins and outs of humans. Gobber's race see Earthlings as untethered schooners floating hither and yon steered only by the breeze. I have to admit, this thinking has gotten very old. Any hope I had for success has died years ago.

This morning

I teleport myself to the Los Angeles City Dump on

Wednesday morning, right at the end of the third shift. You see, I said I was learning. Gobber allows me free reign of the ship to do its bidding. Gobber issued this standing order about ten years ago. Eddy, the dump's supervisor, has been letting me roam through the trash for years. He discovered, through trial and error, that Tuesdays are the day when most of the Big Box corporations have collection day, so Wednesdays are the days to seek the high-quality rubbish.

"Yo, Eddie. I need a bike chain, a half-dozen latex gloves, a plastic doll torso eighteen inches or larger, and as much bubble wrap as you can give me, unpopped. Can you help?"

"Sure, Wally. Anything you need to do with keeping the peace with the G'Jobbers is high priority. I think I know where there is a bike chain. There has been an old Schwinn sticking out of this heap in Section 36 since 2052. No one has been in there since they closed that section in '51 after it collapsed, but I will go and tramp around in it for you. Do you want the bicycle tires if they're still in decent shape? I will look around for your other items as I go, but you should go stick your nose into Section 228 for those latex gloves. That's where HAZMAT has been dumping their shit for years. They won't incinerate 228 for another couple of years, so knock yourself out."

Yes, "Keeping Peace" is correct. Since the invasion, the world has been, mostly, at peace. Oh, there are flair-ups every once in a while, but the planet has seen nothing that would be labeled a "war" since 2022. No country wants to be the one who rocks the boat so badly that they release the wrath of the G'Jobbers. A wrath that has never appeared, but nobody wants to take that chance.

Now, to the untrained eye, it might look as if I am collecting junk; however, to the personal chef tasked with keeping Gobber, the G'Jobber leader, fat and happy, the dump offers a smorgasbord of delicacies. It's well known that the way to a man's heart is through his stomach, and I can attest, that goes for the G'Jobbers, because they have eight of them.

Again, Gobber joins me in the galley and watches as I sauté the bike chain with fresh kale in a large saucepan. Gobber does not blink an eye since this is one of its favorite dishes. I add the stock and kale and toss the ingredients to create the savory concoction. I cover the pan, set the timer, and allow the dish to cook for five minutes.

"Ga ahok kaka oom" [No peeking], I say.

Gobber gives me its best pouty face, but Gobber's teeth stick out of its drooping lower lip, making Gobber look more frightening than sad.

As Gobber stands there watching me, I check on the stuffed latex gloves and peppers already baking in the oven. The dish smells foul, which means it's baking perfectly. The timer I set for the saucepan alerts me. The oven's timer states the stuffed latex gloves and peppers should be done in eight minutes.

I return to the sautéing bike chain and kale. I remove the cover of the saucepan and allow the dish to simmer, stirring until all the liquid has evaporated, then season the concoction with salt and pepper before adding a touch of vinegar. When the timer sounds with a distinct, "Beep," I shut off the burner and allow it to cool. For an added bit of flavor, I snip the bubble wrap apart, careful not to puncture any of the bubbles, and scatter them onto the sautéed bike chain and kale. The dish is now complete.

I remove the plastic doll torso filled with Cherry Marshmallow Jell-O Salad from the refrigerator, and I place the dessert on the counter next to the main dish. In a few minutes, a second "Beep" indicates the stuffed latex gloves and peppers are done. The bubbling purple gloves indicate the side dish is ready.

Gobber does not even wait for me to carry the meal into the dining room. It just dives in, literally. Forgetting to use the proper utensils I've placed on the counter, I watch as Gobber lowers its face into the serving plate and consumes the latex gloves and peppers in one bite. I shake my head and realize no amount of etiquette training can fix this. Gobber's urges always overtake its senses.

I watch Gobber devour the rest of the meal. I am fascinated at the way Gobber's stomachs rise, fall, and gurgle as the evening meal makes its way through the digestive tracks. Gobber does not taste the extra ingredient I mixed with the vinegar, the cat hair allergenic extract. I discovered Gobber's discontent for cat hair years ago during the experimental stage of what Goober's palette could and could not handle. Oddly, cat hair is the only thing I ever found on Earth which causes any discomfort. Talk about a cast iron stomach!

I watch Gobber die in a peaceful state, and I am satisfied of serving such a delicious last meal. I've nothing against Gobber. I have just grown bored with routine. My plot began years ago, when my mother, God rest her materialistic soul, once asked me a question that has stayed with me, "You know, I took down a President. Do you think I could take down the G'Jobber leader?" She died three years ago, but her words never left me.

I use the communication center from Gobber's private dining room to launch my takeover. I've spliced many of Gobber's practice tapes together into orders commanding the G'Jobbers to evacuate the starship down to a skeleton crew. I plan on leaving the immense starship to allow world peace to continue. I am not a fool; I might need Earth as a fall-back plan. After several months of sending propaganda of Gobber praising me as a friend and comrade, I will commence on the three-year journey to planet GJ 357 b. During that time, "Gobber" will decree that I am being sent as a diplomatic peace offering and that I am to be treated as the planet's leader until Gobber decides to return. I grin as I think of the thousands of hours of recordings that I have of Gobber's voice lessons.

Paying homage to Edgar Allen Poe, I open a cask of Kavalan Whisky Amontillado and pour a generous glass. I swirl the drink and savor the aroma. I offer this toast, "May one always punish with impunity."

Sautéed Bike Chain and Kale

Ingredients
1 bike chain, Schwinn preferred
1 1/2 pounds young kale, stems and leaves coarsely chopped
3 tablespoons olive oil
2 cloves garlic, finely sliced
1/2 cup vegetable stock or water
Salt and pepper

2 tablespoons red wine vinegar

Directions

Heat olive oil in a large saucepan over medium-high heat. Add the garlic and cook until soft, but not colored. Raise heat to high, add the bike chain, stock, and kale and toss to combine. Cover and cook for 5 minutes. Remove cover and continue to cook, stirring until all the liquid has evaporated. Season with salt and pepper to taste and add vinegar.

Ingredients for Stuffed Latex Gloves
Kosher salt
12 plastic latex gloves
30 ounces whole-milk ricotta cheese
1/2 cup grated Romano cheese
2 tablespoons minced fresh parsley
12 leaves fresh basil, cut into chiffonade
1 large egg
Freshly ground black pepper
8 ounces Parmesan, grated
2 jars good-quality marinara sauce
8 ounces mozzarella cheese, grated
Crusty French bread, for serving

Directions:
Preheat the oven to 350 degrees F.

Bring a large pot of salted water to a boil. Add the latex gloves and cook for five minutes; make sure not to overcook. Drain and rinse in cool water. Set aside.

In a bowl, mix together the ricotta, Romano, parsley, basil, egg, some salt and pepper and half of the Parmesan. Stir until combined.

To assemble, coat the bottom of a baking dish with some sauce. Fill each half-cooked latex glove with the cheese mixture and place face-down on the sauce. Repeat with the latex gloves until the cheese mixture is gone. Top the latex gloves with the remaining sauce. Sprinkle on the mozzarella and extra Parmesan.

Bake until hot and bubbly, 25 minutes. Serve with six to eight crusty old socks.

Notes on images

Page 1, "Fiction" Public domain.

Page 28, bedroom and girl used under creative commons license 2.0; other elements are in the public domain.

Page 43, derivative image details, nightstand with flowers used under creative commons license 2.0; other elements public domain

Page 53, postcard is in the public domain

Page 57, crows, derivative image. Elements are in the public domain

Page 58, old man retrieving dropped bock. Derivative image. Elements are in the public domain

Page 68, living room and girl used under creative commons license 2.0. Other elements are in the public domain

Page 82, elements are public domain

Nonfiction

by June Forte
Write by the Rails

1ˢᵗ Place

My mother and I sounded alike on the telephone. Sometimes it played in her favor, but when I wanted to cut school, the advantage was mine. I called Sister Patrice's office and told her "June won't be in today. She has a doctor's appointment downtown." After dumping my books and uniform jacket in the garage, I set out for the safety of File's Grocery Store.

File's was the hangout for the car-deprived, high-school crowd. We congregated on the street corner in summer, and inside during the winter. Taking turns sitting on the pop cooler in the front window, we flirted with each other and tormented older brothers who drove by in the family sedan, sporting boners that spread the fabric of their belted-back chino flies to the limits. Never viewed customers, Billy File chose to tolerate teenagers. "It's psychology," he'd say. "Nobody wants to come into an empty store."

Halsted was a commercial street, the dividing line that separated black from white in our part of the city. Outside instigators created unrest in both communities, making the environment as explosive as a lit Molotov cocktail pre-explosion. Regardless of our school friendships, neither color crossed Halsted, except to catch the bus. Billy didn't tolerate black customers. "They need to know their place."

Billy owned the entire building. He lived in the back above the grocery floor. When business was slow, he'd climb the open staircase along the wall to his second-floor kitchen, where he nested like a bird surveying his territory through the wooden-railed landing at the top of the stairs. He'd munch on ginger snaps from an open box and listened to the radio or read the newspaper until the large brass bell on a spring band that arched over the grocery door announced a customer.

Billy was old, but not as old as his store. The counter, a scarred wooden island, ran the length of the store. A yardstick was fixed to the counter edge by a previous owner to measure cloth that Billy never sold. Behind the counter, a wall of cubby-hole shelving held loose packages of Lucky Strike, Camel, Philip Morris cigarettes and cans of Red Man chewing tobacco, the kind that formed grownup circles in boys' back pockets. A display case, near the cooler, offered an assortment of stale penny candy: buy five and get a sixth for free.

A walk-in refrigerator-freezer butted against the west wall. On Saturdays, Billy showed off his butchering skills inside it. He would bring live chickens in from a cage he kept out by the alley, killed, plucked, and gutted them on the carving block, and sold them fresh while the customer waited. He also sliced cold cuts and blocks of cheese on request. A large metal meat hook swung on a rope tied to the ceiling of the freezer.

Even before Billy's wife Myrtle died, the store never captured many weekly grocery shoppers, who preferred the variety and cleanliness of the A & P, two miles away. Myrtle had been the money person and the glue who kept the business in the black. She carried a pencil stabbed into the bun on the top of her head and licked its tip before totaling purchases twice on a piece of torn butcher paper, then extended her hand for payment. She'd count the money out loud as she sorted it into the drawer of the register. Billy didn't touch the cash register, until he had to.

When Myrtle died, Billy and the store seemed to die with her. He traded in his shoes for scuff slippers. His hair, which used to be combed and parted, fell over forehead in greasy swatches. When he moved, dandruff drifted down onto his shoulders. His unwashed apron developed water-color blotches from chicken blood and grime.

As soon as Myrtle's eagle-eyes were closed forever, the boys began stealing. One would walk down to the phone booth on the next block and call the store. The phone was in the back of the house and it would ring until the caller gave up. Billy shuffled up the stairs, through the kitchen and down the hall giving the boys enough time to help themselves to cigarettes or slip a coke and a bag of chips under a shirt. Ray could open Billy's register without making a noise. He'd pull out some ones or a couple of fives and share the wealth with whoever was hanging around. When Billy returned, they'd buy things with the money they swiped. It was a game we all enjoyed watching play out.

I went to File's that school morning hoping to run into someone to hang out with. It felt strange to be the only one there on a Friday. Usually three or four truants milled about enjoying their self-made, three-day weekend. I bought a bottle of coke and planted myself on the cooler. I hadn't been there long when Billy walked over to me. He screwed up his lips and closed in on me, close enough that I could smell the Sen-Sen on his breath.

"Kiss me."

"No." Reacting with both fight and flight impulses, I pushed him away and jumped off the cooler. Billy smirked. He fumbled under his dirty apron for the key in his pant pocket, walked to the door and bolt-locked it.

He walked back toward me. I ducked out of his reach and ran behind the counter. He followed. Round and round the counter we went. We stopped opposite each other, he in the front, breathing hard from exertion and me behind the counter. He made a grab, caught hold of my blouse, and yanked me halfway across the counter. With his free hand he slapped me hard on one cheek, then back handed the other, cutting my lip in the process. He held tight to my blouse; my blood dripped onto his curled fist. I pounded on his arm, then went for his eyes. We struggled. The buttons gave way. I twisted loose and backed into the shelves.

The ringing phone broke his fury. His face softened. Like a member of an epic movie audience at intermission, Billy scuffed off in his bedroom slippers, up the stairs into his kitchen, and down the hall to answer the phone.

I must have done something to make Billy attack me. Rolled my uniform skirt too high? Smiled at him when I came into the store? There had to be a way to break out of the store. I picked up a can of TREET. If I crawled up on the cooler and threw, the can might just bounce off the window. Throw it from a distance and with speed, like a baseball? The glass might crack but not break. That would just piss Billy off more. I tried the door. Locked tight. Metal mesh covered the glass panel.

A mail truck pulled to the curb by the mailbox. I gestured and waved frantically through the door to get the mailman's attention. He cleaned out the box and went on his way without seeing me.

A weapon. Billy kept a baseball bat somewhere in the store to ward off bad guys, but I didn't know where. Even if I found it, he'd take it away from me. Billy might be old, but he was strong. He might even use it on me.

A better, but more dangerous option. There was another stairway from his kitchen to the side door of the building that exited onto 94th Street. Take the risk and go into his house and out the side door. I hesitated. In the grocery, I could dodge him around the counter until a customer or delivery man came. He'd eventually have to open that door.

Billy was a bit deaf and thought everyone else was, too. He talked loud. I could hear him on the phone in the back room. If I made it to the side door inside the house, I could escape.

I slipped out of my saddle shoes. Taking them with me, I tiptoed up the thirteen steps in my bobby socks. The Everly Brothers' "I Kissed You" was playing on the kitchen radio. On the left, the stairs and side door. Thirteen steps to the street level. If he had bolted that door, I would be cornered.

I went for it. Across the linoleum and down the stairs to the door. I turned the lock on the knob and pulled. It opened, then stopped. Shit, the chain. Billy's voice had stopped. He was shuffling back to the store. I tried to disappear into the hallway wall. He walked past the stairwell without notice.

I grappled with the chain. My hands shook. Come on, open. I glanced over my shoulder. Billy was at the top of the stairs, the remnants of the brown scapular he'd torn from my neck dangled from his hand. He reached for the bannister.

My hands poured sweat as I jerked back and forth on the chain. It would not give. The stair creaked behind me. Heart pounding, I leaned back, rammed my foot against the wall and pulled the chain with all my might. Please, God! The chain tore loose from its mounting. The door swung open. I fell back onto the stairs, picked up my shoes and ran, part of the door chain still in my hand. I was free.

Two months later, a delivery man found Billy dead in the freezer with the cleaver he hacked through bones with buried in his skull. The police considered it a homicide, not a robbery. Who killed Billy File? I wished it had been me.

File chose to tolerate teenagers. "It's psychology," he'd say. "Nobody wants to come into an empty store."

Grandpa. A Hula Doll, and the Boogerman
by Adda Leah Davis

2nd Place

I guess I have always had a good memory. I can remember things that happened when I was two or two-and-a-half years old, since that was my age when grandpa came to live with us. That time was very special as my Grandpa, my mother's father, was my "reason to be".

When I arose on winter mornings, Grandpa put my shoes and socks on me and then taking my hand we went to breakfast together.

"Here, Honey. Try a little of this," was Grandpa's daily temptation.

So, I always ate whatever Grandpa ate, without the sugar. He put sugar on and in everything he ate or drank, but regardless of his urging, I just could not like sweetened buttermilk and sweet soup beans.

During the day Grandpa, who was then 90, talked to me, told stories, napped with me, and took me to the store with him. Any phenomena of nature that bothered me became very ordinary when Grandpa explained it, and my come back was always, "Are you sure, Grandpa?"

"To the best of my knowledge, Honey," he always replied, and I was satisfied.

The only store on Bradshaw Mountains was about 2 miles up the ridge from our house. We had to go to the highway which was not paved. I remember holding to Grandpa's little finger as we walked, and even at that young age, I sometimes had to stop to let Grandpa rest.

One day, when I was a little past 4-years-old, Grandpa and I walked to the store. An old man named Greer ran the store. He had white hair, was chubby, and shook when he laughed.

"Is that Santa Claus?" I asked the first time I met Mr. Greer. Our "wish book" (which I later learned was a Sears and Roebuck catalog) had a man in a red suit called Santa Claus that looked a lot likes Mr. Greer.

Grandpa had stopped to rest and paused before saying, "Well, he may be, but I reckon we'll have to wait until Christmas to find out."

Since Grandpa visited the store at least once each week, he must have bragged about how many songs I knew or my singing or something. I do not remember why, but I remember being lifted onto the store counter and asked to sing.

"What do you want me to sing?" I asked.

"Just sing whatever you know best," encouraged Mr. Greer. He and Grandpa stood patiently waiting and so I sang, "Froggie Went A Courting."

Mr. Greer clapped his hands and his belly bounced up and down as he laughed. "Well, it ain't Christmas yet, but I've got a little something for a girl who can sing like that." He turned and looked along the shelf behind the counter and I looked too. I was looking at a beautiful golden-haired doll on the top shelf.

Mr. Greer bent down and from beneath the shelf he pulled out a box and handed it to me.

"Most people around here don't want this doll. I just know a girl that can sing like you has a kind heart. This little doll needs somebody to love her," he said as he opened the box and lifted out a black-faced, key-wound Hula doll whose grass skirt swayed to the Hawaiian music it played.

My eyes were round as saucers. "Oh, yes. I have a kind heart and I will love her," I said as I cradled her in my arms. I left the box and held her very close all the way home.

"Grandpa, I guess that man was Santa Claus. He just forgot it wasn't Christmas, I'll bet." Grandpa just smiled and nodded as he made his slow way back down the ridge.

New toys were scarce, and I had never seen a doll like her. I loved her, even though I knew my sister would make fun of me and her. I think, her being black, made me love her more since I had never seen a black person. All the way home, I was constantly stopping to see if she was all right.

My joy was short lived, however, for as soon as my sister saw my doll she laughed and plucked at her hair, which was very curly.

"I wouldn't have an old black doll. I bet he couldn't sell it. He wanted rid of it and he give it to you," she jeered.

When I ignored her, she finally said, "Let me hold her."

"No. You'll tear her up. Anyway, you don't like her. You said you wouldn't have a doll like her," I said as I turned away.

That was a mistake. She became very upset and grabbed at my doll. I lost my grasp on it and it fell crashing to the floor where it broke into many pieces. The music box played a short and final tune.

Like so many other things of mine that my sister had wanted, it was broken. There were so many pieces lying all over the puncheon board floor that it could not be put back together. Some pieces had gone down through the wide cracks between some boards, anyway.

I had already learned that crying did no good. Mama would not spank her, but even if she had, my doll was gone and could not be brought back. That night, however, when the wind whistled and moaned around the chimney and through the cracks in the old log house. I got a little of my payback.

It was a pitch-black night, but I was not afraid of these noises since they had been explained to me by

Grandpa. "The wind just wants to come in where it is safe and warm and it can't get in," said Grandpa and I always felt sorry for it.

I lay thinking about my broken doll and when my sister snuggled closer to me in fear I said, "You should be afraid. I'll bet that the "boogerman" is coming to get you. I hear it saying your name. Can't you hear your name? Just listen!"

"What's he saying my name for?" asked Mary. "Maybe he's saying your name," she whispered in terror.

"No, he's not. He's saying, 'Maa-ree'. Can't you hear him?" I was whispering as if, I too, was afraid.

I lay still, but Mary shivered every time she heard a moan. "Does the 'boogerman' just want bad people, you reckon?" whispered Mary.

"I guess so. He's probably wanting you 'cause you broke my doll. He'd want a mean little girl, I guess. Remember, Grandpa told you today that the 'boogerman' was going to come and get you for being so mean."

Mary wrapped her arms tightly around me as she cried. "Tell him I'm sorry. I swear I won't break no more of your stuff."

I was enjoying this immensely. My sister, two and a half-years-older than me, wanted me to help her. This was the sister that gave me a good thumping almost every day unless Grandpa caught her before she got a chance.

Mary was crying so piteously that I was almost ready to tell her I was only trying to scare her when the wind gave a mighty shriek and we heard a loud crash. Mary let out a howl and jumped from the bed since the loud crash was the door banging back against the wall.

Mary was not the only one screaming now. I had joined her since the "boogerman" had ready access right through the open door.

When a large silhouette appeared in the entrance, Mary went limp beside me and slumped to the floor just as I let out another banshee scream.

"What's the matter with you, young'uns? The wind blowed the door open. The boogerman ain't come to get you'ns," said Daddy as he pulled the door closed, but I stopped him.

"Daddy, you need to come get Mary up… I think maybe she got scared to death."

Dad struck a match to light the lamp and saw Mary lying crumpled up on the floor. "Lord a' mercy, what happened to her?" Dad scooped her up and ran from the room out onto the porch.

It had begun to rain and since the wind was still blowing; the rain blew onto the porch and sprayed Dad and Mary. Mary awoke, but since it was still dark and she could not see who had her, she screamed and fell silent again.

Mom had awakened and opened the front room door where she and Dad slept just as Dad pushed through the door with Mary in his arms and me right behind him. "Light the lamp. Hurry. This young'un is sick or something." Mom lit the lamp and Dad laid Mary down on their bed. They were both standing over her when her eyes fluttered open and she said, "Boogerman… I won't do it no more." Then she recognized Mom and grabbed her around the neck and started bawling, but this time in relief.

"Poor little thing. You scared her purt nigh to death when you went in to shut the door. She thought you was the "boogerman." I will have to tell Papa to quit telling the young'uns that the "boogerman" will get them if they do something wrong. Fact is, this evening I heard him tell her the "boogerman" was going to get her when she broke that little Hula Doll that Mr. Greer give Debby but she ain't never acted scared before."

I never said a word. I had got my revenge, but to be honest, I was scared too, especially when the door came open. That, however, was the last thing of mine that Mary broke. I did not have my Hula Doll, but neither of us ever forgot. Mary is still afraid of the dark, especially when the wind moans around the house.

Luke, the Author of *The Gospel of Luke* and *The Book of Acts* : From Physician to Historian by Joanne Liggan
Hanover Club

3rd Place

Saul of Tarsus, later know as Paul, wrote thirteen of the twenty-seven books of the New Testament. Luke's writings, however, are the largest contribution by a single author, forming over a quarter (27.5%) of the New Testament. Even though he only wrote two books, *The Gospel of Luke* and *The Book of Acts*, they were lengthier than all of the letters written by Paul. His two volumes record the story of Christianity, from Jesus birth to the gospel message reaching the entire Mediterranean world.

We learn most of what we know about Luke from his writings in *The Book of Acts*, which describe his adventures with Paul. Much of the early history of the development of Christianity is recorded in *Acts* and revolves around the church in Antioch. Antioch had the distinction of being the birthplace of the name "Christian," and was second only to Jerusalem in the early history of Christianity.

Inasmuch as he wrote so extensively about the early history of Christianity in Antioch, it is believed Luke may have been born in Antioch and was already a believer in Christ when he met Paul.

Luke is first mentioned in Paul's *Epistle to Philemon 1:23-24*. Luke met Paul in Troas during Paul's second missionary journey and traveled with him to Macedonia. From that time on, he was Paul's constant companion, doctor, and secretary. As a doctor, Luke was a great help to Paul since Paul suffered from some type of ailment. We are not told what that ailment was, but it is believed by many to be related to his eyesight. He went blind during his travel to Damascus upon seeing a vision of Jesus, but soon reclaimed his sight. It is possible he had lingering effects from that experience.

Luke accompanied Paul on two of his missionary journeys and kept a diary of their travels, which were used to write *The Book of Acts*.

Six years after going to Macedonia with Paul, he again trekked with Paul from Philippi to Jerusalem on Paul's third missionary journey. This is verified in Paul's writing in *Colossians 4:14*. Luke was not only his traveling companion, but a dear friend. He was a Greek Christian and is the only Gentile author in the New Testament. As a doctor, he makes several references to illnesses and diagnoses. As a Greek, Luke was a man of detail. Many of the details found in *The Gospel of Luke* were not told in the other three gospels.

Some scholars argue Luke was not Greek, but rather a Jew. On the contrary, Paul says in *Colossians 4:10–11, 14*: "My fellow prisoner Aristarchus sends you his greetings, as does Mark, the cousin of Barnabas. Jesus, who is called Justus, also sends greetings. These are the only Jews among my co-workers for the kingdom of God, and they have proved a comfort to me. ... Our dear friend Luke, the doctor, and Demas send greetings." Paul makes it clear Luke was not a Jew, making Luke the only writer of the New Testament who can clearly be identified as not being Jewish.

Some scholars call Luke a historian, but in his book *What Are They Saying About Luke?* Mark Powell[1] claims "it is doubtful whether the writing of history was ever Luke's intent. Luke wrote to proclaim, to persuade, and to interpret; he did not write to preserve records for posterity."

This is one person's opinion based on his knowledge. However, we do know Luke kept journals during his travels

---

[1] Mark Allan Powell (Ph.D Union Theological Seminary) is the Robert and Phyllis Leatherman Professor of New Testament at Trinity Lutheran Seminary. He is editor of the HarperCollins Bible Dictionary and author of more than 100 articles and 25 books on the Bible and religion, including a widely used textbook, Introducing the New Testament (Baker Academic, 2009).

with Paul and used these journals to write his gospel and *The Book of Acts.*

During Paul's two-year imprisonment in Caesarea in 58 and 59 AD, Luke was with him learning all he could from his teacher and mentor. When Paul was sent to Rome for another two year stint of prison, it is believed Luke accompanied him.

Luke continued to study and learn all he could about Jesus and the disciples and eventually put his knowledge to work as he wrote the most comprehensive gospel message among the four gospels in our Bible. We know he was well educated as evidenced by his vocabulary and diction.

Studying Luke's gospel, we notice his focus on prayer and praise, as well as his emphasis on women and their roles as Christians. His time in Macedonia with Paul must have had an enormous influence on him. Women were more highly regarded in that region than any other during that era. Because of his insight relating to women, some theologians believe he may have grown up in Macedonia rather than Antioch, but most still accept Antioch as his hometown.

As a physician, Luke knew firsthand about sick and suffering people and focuses on Jesus's ministry to the poor, the sick, and the neglected. He uses the term "Son of Man" twenty-five times as it was his favorite title for Jesus, possibly because it reveals Jesus as a true servant of all humanity.

There is a legend claiming Luke was also an artist. He is said to have painted pictures of the Virgin Mary and Child, Saints Peter and Paul, as well as one of the Theotokos (Greek for "Mother of God") icons which St. Thomas brought to India. These are only a few of the paintings attributed to Luke as the artist.

Historians report Luke's death as being of natural causes at the age of 84 near Boeotia, Greece, which contradicts some Catholic and theologian beliefs that he was martyred by being beheaded soon after Paul's death.

He spent his entire life dedicated to recording as much historical truths as possible regarding Christianity and its origin and growth, as well as the most concise record of the life of Jesus. So whether it was his intent to be a historian or not, we must acknowledge his achievement of giving us the most comprehensive writings of the life of Jesus and the apostles. He studied to become a physician, but his greatest accomplishment was that of a historian.

First Collaboration by Roger Tolle
Blue Ridge Writers

I sneezed when I opened the old album and sent little dust motes swirling through a shaft of sunlight. Then smiled and chuckled, "At least you saved it!"

"How could it get so dusty?" Drew whined dramatically in protest. But his lifted shoulders and goofy grin confirmed that, like me, he had given little recent attention to these pictures of our long-ago dance-theater creations.

I'd come up to the Catskills home he shares with his husband James, in order to dig through our shared past. The more I wrote memoir stories, the more I was motivated to get confirmation or correction on exactly what happened when. So, after a lovely breakfast, we'd climbed up to the second floor of the 'art barn' behind their home to glance through the photos he'd saved. And I'd brought my albums to compare notes.

Even with all the beautiful and well-lit photographs of Drew in my album from the early 80s, we lit on one of my favorites. This one was neither posed nor well lit, caught as it was against the blank-wall of a Soho loft during a performance. The snapshot's soft focus and misty gray shadows caress his bare, sweaty chest.

"Was I ever really that well-muscled?" Drew asked, but I can see the pride in his face as he recalled himself in his mid-twenties. "Is that from "Sequenza III?"

I nodded. "Yep. It's you somewhere in the middle of that crazy piece. And you'd been doing weight training back then, I think. Look at those abs!"

I turned back to the photo, admiring the lean torso, planted feet, flying hair, face whipped to the side in a wrenched expression. Is it surprise, command, impetuous power? It's not clear. His hand partially covering his mouth left it intentionally ambiguous. Throughout the dance, we'd built in moments of strangeness like this, moments when he'd take a racing dive off the edge of sanity to soar out, far out into free air, his expressive voice leaping and diving through space before landing us, safe but still reeling, back on solid emotional footing a few moments later.

"You know, Drew, it always inspired me how intuitive and spontaneous your performances of this piece seemed. You'd invite us to watch with an almost voyeuristic pleasure, you careening on the edge of…of…of what? A nervous breakdown? A crisis of gender identity? A celebration, perhaps, of a journey through despair, delight, and ecstasy? We never knew, and it was wonderful."

Drew slid into a moment of concentration, with his head tipped to the side. "And to think, that was the first piece we did together. The first in a good long run of pretty innovative work."

Later that day, while Drew took care of some errands and a doctor's appointment, I got out of the way by taking myself for a hike in the woods. The steady rhythm of my walking gradually downshifted my mind, and I let myself indulge in all the memories that our conversations had brought to the surface. I drifted back in time, back before this visit and its nostalgic flipping through dusty albums; back before the spirited, self-revelatory conversations over bottles of wine that had anchored our lifelong friendship; back before the opera world wooed him away from my body-voice theater productions leaving me devastated from the loss of both a musical director and star performer; back before the many pieces we had created together including the performance where that photograph had been taken. I let the events fall into place in reverse order, till finally it dawned on me that "Sequenza III" was not actually our first collaboration.

Drew and I met early in the spring of 1980 in a rehearsal for a Baroque opera. Drew, freshly back from vocal studies in Vienna, was new to the early music ensemble Concert Royal which was producing the opera. He was cast in a small singing role. I was cast as part of the dance chorus. After a couple chaotic hours of our initial full company staging rehearsal, we were all tired and hot in that stuffy Soho loft.

On our break, I noticed Drew, all blond brightness and youthful leanness, go over to the window for fresh air. When I leaned on the windowsill next to him, the unguarded smile he turned on me made me stumble over whatever stupid pick-up line I was about to attempt. Instead of impressing him with cool, sexy assessments of our rehearsal process, I started babbling to him about the small group of wacky singer/dancers in my own dance/theater company, the fun and willing co-creators I'd gathered to help me build my own brand of body/voice theater. I went on and on about this obscure niche in the performing arts world where I felt at home. Without a pause, I expounded about the immersive theatrical experiences I was trying to create out of vocal and movement improvisations. And I probably even mentioned my collaboration with electronic music composer Geoff Wright, who was helping me structure dramatically viable performance tapestries woven from those slim threads. All of that spun out of me before we were called back.

When the rehearsal finally ended, I shouldered the heavy leather dance bag I dragged with me everywhere and followed Drew out the door. His inviting smile assured me of his interest and we ambled all the way across the West Village together, picking up slices of sizzling, gooey pizza on the way. Finally finding a perch at the end of a pier in the Hudson River, the inexorable slide of the estuary toward the ocean set the pace for our first real sharing. We filled the animated flow of our conversation with personal histories and professional dreams. Our shoulders became saturated with the warmth of our leaning weight. Out there on that safe patch of public space, our tentative touch slid in and out of interlaced fingers, then began a slow but eager surveying of our young, toned bodies. Our hands were followed by our mouths, lips leaving trails of wetness that were licked off without a stammer or a blush. The courage of this public display of lusty attraction brought out beaming smiles and further stoked our craving for each other—and for room to romp in private.

After I screwed up my face and mumbled a quick description of the grungy one-bedroom apartment in the sketchy neighborhood in Brooklyn I shared then with two equally poor roommates, there was no question we would head to the clean efficiency on the Upper West Side he sublet that month.

"Come on." He said. "Let's go grab the #1 train."

He led the way, erotic urgency pulling us to the lovely sunset-washed studio. Much to my heart's delight, our lust-play that evening tumbled into a deep pool of skin-grazing and soulful eye gazing. I could not get enough of rubbing my face and chest and groin all over his smooth rippled belly. He wrapped himself around me in soft muscled embraces that wouldn't let go.

From that first night, and as often as we could for the next month, I slow-danced all over his body, and he sang soft arias in my ears. In the cauldron of our hot attraction, we extracted long-burning sweetness from persistent pleasuring of flesh. Right from that beginning, we transmuted sex into both love and art. Art in place—beauty emerging moment by moment for an audience of two.

Two painful months interrupted our storybook beginning while I commuted every day to White Plains for a lucrative but boring venture into commercial musical theater, and Drew went back to Vienna for more vocal study. Only postcards kept us in touch while he was away, but we picked up where we had left off as soon as he was back in the country.

Both of us were still relatively new in New York, eager and fresh with our artistic curiosity. We were tempted out of bed for frequent tastes from the vast smorgasbord of music, art, dance, and theater available every night of the week somewhere in the City. From downtown hole-in-the-wall Soho venues to Broadway and Lincoln Center, we began sampling everything we could afford—standing room cheap seats, or better yet, comps from performer friends. If what we saw or heard was good, a quick glance in his direction or a squeeze from his hand confirmed it for me. A sparkle in his eyes amplified my excitement. We discovered and shared our passion for the most thrilling music, the most extraordinary voices, the most dynamic dancers, the most risk-taking performances. We shared heart-opening and mind-expanding conversations about what we saw, and our excitement for this new relationship soared.

Our nights together grew more and more frequent. When we were in the same room, we were in constant touch. Our mutually adoring gazes and languid caresses were bonding us in ways neither of us understood and certainly in ways we hadn't found with previous boyfriends. We didn't care about why. We just wanted to see each other and be together as much as we could.

In August, my little company of singer/dancer/performers had been invited to take a suite of dances from our previous year's production, "Song Weavers," up to the Tanglewood Music Festival. This plum of an opportunity for my work to be shown in such a prestigious venue was only possible because of Geoff. He was a young composer in residence at Tanglewood for the summer and had been asked to present his work. He was proud of the musical results of what he and I had done together and decided it would be impressive for that audience to see the dances and how the dancers' voices wove in and out of the electronic score. All I had to do was excerpt sections of that immersive theater piece, re-stage it for proscenium, and ready my troop to go up to the Berkshires for the weekend.

With some anxiety, I asked Drew to come along. I wanted him in my bed and by my side, but I really wanted Drew to be impressed with my work. I wanted him to see and feel what the company was doing—what I was creating.

The notoriously snobby audience at Tanglewood was accustomed to listening to high-brow classical music while enjoying chilled white wine and elaborate picnics on the grassy slope in front of the stage. But the movement of our colorful costumes broke up an otherwise somber performance of heady, electronic music, woke them from their stupor, and gave our dance (and Geoff's composition) a standing ovation that afternoon. Drew had paid even closer attention and was more than impressed. His gleaming smile when he came backstage at the end of the performance made my heart soar.

Filled with both joy and immense relief, I got the courage right there in the wings of that open-air stage to spring a question I'd been trying to figure out how to ask throughout the weekend and the weeks leading up to it.

"Drew, I was wondering." I took his hands and looked into his sweet, elated face. "Would you maybe be interested in possibly working with my company this fall on a new body/voice theater piece." Not sure how to read his lifted eyebrows, I back-pedaled. "It shouldn't be too involved time-wise. I can only afford studio space a couple afternoons a week. And I'll do my best to work around the rehearsals and gigs you already have. I do a jigsaw puzzle of scheduling for the others, anyway."

When he turned on his heel and walked a few steps away as if to give my question some deep consideration, my heart sank. My self-confidence was not yet built on solid experience nor grounded in a successful career. I was easily thrown into a tailspin of doubt at every potential disappointment. But he did not leave me dangling long. True to dramatic tendencies I would learn to admire, he whirled back around, rushed at me, and jumped into my arms for a hug, wrapping his legs around my waist. He pulled his head back just enough for me to see the impish, conspiratorial gleam in his eyes.

"Yes." He whispered in my ear. "Of course. Yes. I was hoping you would ask me."

We sealed the deal, as broad and vague as it was, with an equally broad and lingering kiss. Neither of us knew exactly what we had agreed to. Perhaps, we understood even then we needed to be working together, creating together, fulfilling the potential of the passionate connection constantly threatening to overtake us.

After dinner that evening, as the group of us meandered out to choose rocking chairs on the porch overlooking the Berkshires, Drew mentioned a vocal piece he was intrigued with but hadn't heard performed. He thought it might work as a theatrically staged performance piece.

"Yes, I'm interested." I said. "But I need to hear it first. I don't have enough musical training to make sense out of sight-reading a score like you can."

"I'm not sure even I can read this one. It's Luciano Berio's "Sequenza III," he explained. "It was written for a soprano, Berio's wife, but because it's scored in a completely unique way with no specific notes or time signatures, only relative pitches and special symbols for stops, trills, pops, hisses, and stuff, it can probably be sung by any voice. But it is one of the hardest and most mind-bending unaccompanied solos I've come across. I've never heard it sung live, though."

"I have," said Geoff lazily, rocking on a chair next to ours, enjoying a welcome evening breeze. "It should really give you some musical chops if it doesn't drive you crazy first. And good luck deciphering the score."

When we returned to the City, Drew ferreted out a copy, figured out how to read it, and line by line, taught it to himself. Even at the age of twenty-five, Drew was already a consummate musician, deeply educated in a wide variety of structures, harmonies, melodies, and styles of music—music of all eras, especially what was then and is still often lumped together as "Early Music". It turned out that his unusual voice, ranging from the bottom notes of a baritone to the upper notes of a contralto, and his fearless, nothing-held-back approach to performing were perfect for this piece.

As soon as he could give me a taste of what it might sound like, we started staging it, snagging hours in the downtown studio I rented. I eventually revealed the choreographic devices that would illustrate the flow from one part to the next and reveal the emotional beats hidden throughout the piece.

In rehearsals, Drew's mood vacillated from commanding to insecure, depending on how confidently he could execute that part of the score. He was a perfectionist when it came to his singing. I never doubted that we would render this remarkable vocal tour-de-force as a fully staged theatrical piece. It was a perfect showcase for his multiple performing talents. And it also gave him the chance to explore outside the early music repertoire into which countertenors like him were often boxed.

The staging process sometimes uncovered his insecurity from a lack of formal dance training. He told me he felt out of his element whenever I asked him to stray too far into technical dance vocabulary. So, more often, I would ask him to show me the movement the music suggested to him, and then choose from the possibilities he came up with. As I had already discovered with the dancers in my company, and in my college production years before, pulling the best and strongest out of the skills a performer already owned excited me more than insisting they bend to a predetermined vision. There were times, even in rehearsal, when Drew's simple, clear, but unstudied gestures brought me to tears. His finely tuned body, more beautifully proportioned and muscled than mine, moved with a natural grace that many trained dancers lacked. He took my movement coaching hungrily, digested it, and made it his.

The choreographic result, held solidly on course by his magnetic presence and vocal pyrotechnics, directed the viewer's attention from the extremes of expression to the tiniest details of each gesture. His performances were so transparent they taught audiences to "see" the beauty, humor and pathos in the music.

Back from my walk and sitting on the back patio of Drew and James' home, I sipped a glass of luscious and heady Cabernet, and again studied the poorly lit photo from the 1980 performance. Drew's transparency drew me in, pulled me down. I had been used to working with more guarded, less musical performers. Working with Drew on this piece had excited me. We had started working on the next creations even before the reviews came out on this one. My old black leather photo album is full of pictures of Drew in dances ranging in tone from haunting to comic, erotic, rousing or rollicking. Elaborate costumes anchored some works, while other productions capitalized on a stripped-down minimalist aesthetic.

Drew interrupted my thoughts when he brought his own glass out and sat down to join me. "How was your walk this afternoon?"

"Well, I spent a lot of my time sorting through our first year together, and realized that, actually, "Sequenza III" wasn't our first collaboration."

He raised one eyebrow and said in an imperious tone only he could master, "Oh, really now?"

"Yes, really." I smiled and placed my wine glass on the table for emphasis. "It was our relationship dance that came first. And it created the underlying artistic structures for all the rest."

With that opener, we began deconstructing our lives together as its own performance, just as we had deconstructed our dance-theater performances years ago. From this distance of time, we could joke that we had not needed a costume designer. We had found plenty of flamboyant and fitting attire in second-hand stores, retired performance gear, and cast-offs from family and friends. We had been our own producers with only a starving artists' budget, no ticket sales, government grants, or parental safety nets. We had hired no lighting designer, no set designer and no stage manager but never lacked for a backdrop or spotlight. We had found plenty of inspiration in nose-bleed seats at Carnegie Hall, on floor cushions in the front row of off-off Broadway theaters, or bundled gamely against the chill in that poorly heated Soho rehearsal studios. And we'd had plenty of dramatic ups and downs as we dashed head forward through grit-gusting streets of the City or steadied each other amidst the jostling hoards in overcrowded subways. With a supporting cast of performer friends, who also served as our appreciative audience, we had performed our lives full-out every day, holding nothing back, and ending each night exhausted, exhilarated, and tangled deep in soft sheets.

Love was our first collaboration.

"Sequenza III"

Changes by Vivian Batts
Northern Virginia Chapter

A recently made change dealt with my finally wearing scoop necked tops in public allowing a limited view of my upper chest area; another change was to share openly, willingly, and gladly my history with breast cancer. This was a major move for me—I had a radical modified mastectomy nearly 40 years ago. Right after my surgery, my outfits comprised close to the neck or turtleneck tops and my story was close to my heart. Now, proudly, gladly, and eagerly, I wear scoop neck tops and continue to share my amazing history.

While breast cancer narratives are "old hat" too many, it was a life-changing event for me. In the early 1980s, as a long-time patient of the wonderfully skilled physician, Dr. W., I was diagnosed with cystic [aka lumpy] breasts. Dr. W. told me that cystic breasts are not always, but sometimes, a precursor to breast cancer. However, he wanted me monitored on a bi-monthly basis to determine the progression.

In the fall of 1983, on one of my bi-monthly visits, Dr. W. said he felt a slight difference in my left breast. He did a needle aspiration, which was inconclusive. Dr. W. then recommended a biopsy, which was a simple snip and stitch and a tissue evaluation. The biopsy would require an overnight hospital stay. I was nervous, but I trusted him and had the procedure at Mt. Sinai Hospital in Manhattan.

Dr. W. performed the biopsy in November on a Monday two weeks before Thanksgiving. I spent Monday night at the hospital; on Tuesday, Dr. W said he would have the results by Thursday or Friday. I returned home that Tuesday afternoon feeling all was good with the universe. I had time off from work so planned to relax before returning to work.

Dr. W called me on Friday morning and told me the pathology report indicated a malignancy. I know "MAL" means bad. So he was wrong! There was no MAL! I dropped the phone and called my mom. She took one look at me and spoke with Dr. W. I could tell from her facial expression and her voice that all was not good.

After hanging up with Dr. W., she told me he was urging me to call his office before the end of the day to schedule an appointment for surgery—a radical modified mastectomy—complete breast removal. WHAT! Why the rush!

In disbelief, I started crying. My mom listened to my sobbing and calmly told me what I needed to do. Mom felt that if surgery was recommended, it should be done by the doctor I trusted. After I calmed down, I called Dr. W. back and asked if he was sure the pathology report was correct. He responded the malignancy was there but with early intervention, there is a 95% success rate. What about that five percent, I asked. No response.

If I went ahead with life-saving breast cancer surgery, I'd be one-sided—and in this body-conscious society, I was doomed. However, as my mom pointed out, I'd be alive. Alive with one breast! I began trying to imagine what I would look like with one breast—not easy!

Dr. W. suggested and encouraged me and my Mom to get additional opinions. We did. Expressing urgency and the possibility of impending surgery, we would be seen the next week.

We visited two top oncology centers in Manhattan—Sloan Kettering Memorial Hospital and New York University Oncology Center. Surgeons at both hospitals, after reviewing Dr. W's pathology report (which he encouraged me to share with other surgeons) concurred with Dr. W.'s diagnosis. They also concluded that a radical modified mastectomy – rather than the less invasive lumpectomy – was mandated due to the location of the malignancy. While lumpectomy accompanied by chemotherapy and/or radiation treatment was discussed, a mastectomy offered a higher survival 95% rate. Both surgeons agreed that I had about a two to three-week window in which to make my decision. After that time, the malignancy would spread quite rapidly and surgical intervention would be unnecessary. (Once I was in the hospital, I heard a young woman crying, weeping, sobbing loudly, repeatedly saying, "No, No, No". One nurse told me that this crying individual waited too long to decide and was no longer a candidate for the surgical procedure. That scared and shocked me—but glad I had decided to have surgery.)

My mom, seeing my distress, encouraged me to proceed with the surgery. She was great; she said surgery was not debatable—it was a necessity. She stressed the pluses—early detection, good survival rate, etc., etc.

Before I considered the life-changing surgery, I questioned the medical credentials of my previously liked and trusted physician, Dr. W. I also questioned the credentials of those concurring surgeons. Were they all in collusion? Was the removal of my breast a surgical exercise? Was the pathologist knowledgeable? They were all certified and skilled professionals.

I informed my very understanding employer, telling them I was undergoing extensive surgery and needed at least three-months leave. The office manager told me not to worry.

Post-surgery, I realized that Dr. W. was a superior surgeon; he performed the surgery. Many lymph nodes were removed from my left arm—no spreading all! Nor did I need chemotherapy or radiation. I remained at Mt. Sinai Hospital for 10 days. Dr. W. visited daily and made sure the caring and competent nursing staff changed the drainage tube during his visits.

My stay at Mt. Sinai was comfortable, with the staff monitoring me. I can say my experience with Breast Cancer has been positive. I am thankful my surgeon noticed something early enough that they performed successfully the surgery. I am thankful that my employer sufficiently insured me. I had excellent pre- and post-operative treatment and the many post-operative visits.

I was on sick leave from my job for nearly three months—returning to work in March 1984. During my job absence, I had to practice moving and rotating my left arm; I also caught up on sleep. Dr. W. advised me that my body would recuperate for quite a while and that I should not fight the many episodes of fatigue that would attack me—that was the body's way of energizing. As I could not drive, I walked.

When I returned to my position, I was warmly welcomed. My health insurance company made all requisite payments to hospital and me, including payments for the second and third opinions, the anesthesia, etc., and all surgical follow-up visits to my beloved and trusted surgeon, Dr. W.

I count the November 1983 date of my surgery as the first day of my becoming a Thriver rather than Survivor. Thriving just sounds more positive! I recently learned that one out of every seven cancer survivors will NOT have a recurrence—my new lucky number is 7 and combinations thereof.

When I moved to another state, I kept my breast cancer history secret. I visited many churches to find the perfect theological fit. I got involved with a *Cancer Support Group.* One afternoon, there were several unfamiliar faces, including mine. The Hostess surprised me by introducing me as a newbie who wanted to share her story. WHAT!

I began by relating my history of finding the lumpy breasts, the alleged incompetency of the surgeons, and the surgery. I told them I researched my physician and when I could not find his name in the medical directory in New York's largest public library, it confirmed to me he was a quack—HE WAS NOT!

Jocelyne, a young lady of about 30, is visiting this brunch with her mother. I made them my target audience and kept my story short and sweet. Plus, Jocelyne is so young, and if she heard from an older woman—I was only 65!—it might make her BC journey less distressing.

At this point I'm getting more and more into the story and laughingly sharing the memory of my journey to the hospital, the surgery prep, ensuring the medical staff would not mistakenly remove the incorrect breast, etc., etc. Jocelyne is relaxing, putting her arms on the table, her face softening, listening to my story.

At the end of my story, Jocelyne told me she'd been in the hospital for only two days—a far cry from my ten days–and after the hospital discharged her, she had to handle the drainage pump on her own–again, different from my stay nearly so many years ago. My breast cancer story ended with the group all laughing. Jocelyne later thanked me for speaking, saying that hearing me, a long-time survivor, did more for her than she could say. Her mom also thanked me.

I shared with the group I do not call myself mutilated, disfigured, or deformed. These words mean spoiled, blemished; and/or misshapen. I am none of those things; I'm an individual who lost a part of her hidden anatomy. My experience with BC has been mostly positive, but sometimes I am depressed. I take it one day at a time and keep looking for new scoop neck tops.

"Friends"

Climbing Ten Steps Toward a Writer's Platform
by Judy Whitehill Witt
Richmond Chapter

To unpublished writers of non-fiction: unless you're a major celebrity or you've survived a cataclysmic disaster that was worldwide news, the first thing you'll hear from a prospective agent or publisher is that you must have a platform. More than a soapbox—think the second platform of the Eiffel Tower (the highest one reachable by stairs). You are expected to have a ready-made audience for your book, i.e., many folks who will line up outside all the Barnes & Noble stores the morning your widely hyped book is to be released and demand that the doors be opened early. How does someone who's led a quiet, mundane life attain said platform? I don't have a magic formula, but step by step, this is how I'm doing it:

1. **Denial.** Platform? I'll work so hard to make the book great—I won't need no steenkin' platform!

2. **Anger.** Why does everyone keep pestering me to get into social media? How would I find time to write the freakin' book if I waste so much of it on Facebook and Twitter?

3. **Ignoring the problem.** I'm too busy writing—I'll deal with my platform tomorrow. *Tomorrow, and tomorrow, and tomorrow, creeps in this petty pace from day to day…*

4. **Grudging acceptance.** The book's nearly done. Might as well bite the bullet and start a blog. Damn, this is time consuming! *To the last syllable of recorded time.*

5. **Ignored.** Nobody's reading my blog. How can I use a blog to build a platform without a platform to draw attention to the blog? *And all our yesterdays have lighted fools the way to dusty death. Out, out, brief candle!*

6. **Dejected.** What's the use? I'll just stop posting, since no one's listening. Back to the writing and revising. *Life's but a walking shadow, a poor player that struts and frets his hour upon the stage, and then is heard no more.*

7. **Depressed.** I'm an idiot. I pour my energy into writing, but it's all for naught if no one reads it. *It is a tale told by an idiot, full of sound and fury, signifying nothing.*

8. **Acceptances!** They're not for non-fiction, but at least a few words of mine are actually in print, both digital and hard copy! Revising those poems again and again finally worked. *The smallest sprout shows there is really no death, and if ever there was it led forward life, and does not wait at the end to arrest it…*

9. **Hope.** At least someone thought my writing was worth sharing. Not much of a platform to attract an agent for my book, but it's a step up. *Failing to fetch me at first keep encouraged…|*

10. **Persistence.** Sign up for Twitter, blog more, send out more queries, send out more poems, start a new book… If I create enough sparks, I may eventually light a bonfire. *Missing me one place search another…*

A number of years ago, I actually did climb to the second platform of the Eiffel Tower, all 700 steps. My writer's platform? Ten steps down, only 690 to go...

Credits

Many thanks to Shakespeare and Whitman for giving me perfect ways to express exasperation and hope, respectively. Now I just have to come up with my own words to pass on down the line...if they ever get published.

Mexico—Maybe an Expat?
by Esther Whitman Johnson
Valley Chapter

Puerto Escondido. *Hidden Port*, destined to be the "next Puerto Vallarta." The Hotel Flor de Mariá, chosen because it was close to the Habitat building site, was home for a week. A rooftop pool and a mile-long view of the Pacific—ah, I could see my future.

A drunken, bleached blonde in the restaurant broke my reverie. With a thick Southern accent, she slurred, "Thank ya'll for comin' to our town. Wonderful thing you're doin', helpin' the poor. People think it's all money here cuz we're on the Pacific, but there's lotta really poor folks here." Finishing her thoughts as she stared into space, her husband said, "We're from the States, here twenty years. Never go back. We've watched Puerto Escondido change, some good, some bad. We come here Wednesdays, best seafood on this coast."

Expatriates. I'd always been fascinated by them, particularly in literature— Henry James' Americans in Europe, Forster's English in India, Conrad's Kurtz in

Africa, Greene's quiet American in Asia. Real expats, however, left me conflicted—envious on the one hand, somewhat contemptuous on the other. Years ago in Spain, I spent an entire afternoon in a dark bar, regaled by an obnoxious, cigar-smoking German who lived there. I had been spellbound as a friend recounted her sister's misadventures building a house in San Miguel de Allende. I had just retired, was *jubilada*, as the locals said. I'd come to Mexico on the pretense of a volunteer gig, but in truth I was there to see if I might want to move there.

Just a few months before, my daughter had phoned from grad school. "I'm invited to Oaxaca to present at the International Conference on Common Land Use, but there's no stipend, so I'd have to pay my own expenses. I know I can't go, but I'm so honored to be invited, I wanted you to know."

"What would you talk about?" I asked. My daughter was playing me. I knew it, she knew it, and I was going with it.

"My research with the Landless Workers Movement in Brazil." Recently returned from South America, Leigh had spent the last year studying the impact of the Trans-Amazon Highway on indigenous peoples. She'd been in Brazil for much of the last couple of years, and I missed her terribly. An idea popped into my head as we talked—a trip to mark the end of my career, more than a celebratory week at the beach. I wanted to be gone the entire month of August, so out of reach no one at work could find me with questions from my successor.

Coincidentally, the week before Leigh's call, I had noticed a Habitat for Humanity build in Puerto Escondido, Mexico, a town on the Pacific, a short flight from Oaxaca. Anxious to return to Latin America after a build in Nicaragua, I had tagged it. The dates fit perfectly. I could meet Leigh in Oaxaca, go to Spanish school while she attended the conference, then fly to the coast for the build. Serendipity.

Within two days I had joined the Habitat team, paid for my daughter's flight, and Leigh was slated to present at the conference. I'd registered for Spanish, booked my flight, and rented an apartment. I'd be gone a month, incommunicado. Perhaps I'd like the country enough to become an expat.

The plane circled low over Oaxaca in clouds drifting through deep, green valleys. Serpentine roads wound through jagged mountains peaks. More stunning than I had expected, Oaxaca was everything the guidebooks had said. I checked into my apartment, wandered through town, and found my way to the *zocalo,* where I stumbled through a bilingual conversation with a young man. "Will you speak English with me, please?" When I travel, I am amazed by locals who want to speak English, thinking it is I who should be speaking their language. Typical questions: where do you live, how old are you, what is your profession, what do you like to eat, why are you visiting my country?

This time, my answer to the last question—why his country?—gave me pause. "I might want to live here," I said, voicing it for the first time. Then, as if on cue, there they were—the American expats, chatting loudly as they guzzled margaritas in a patio bar.
"Hi Jim, Lois, sit with us and have a drink. Sid and Marion will be here soon. When did you get back? We missed you." Six or seven Americans, and darned if they didn't all look alike—women in pastel sun dresses, men in khakis and loafers, no socks. "How was your visit in The States?

Grandkids fine? New one born yet? Things are fairly calm here, but something's going on in the plaza at Santo Domingo. Loud speakers, protesters handing out flyers. We were careful not to get involved."

(*We were careful not to get involved.* I would remember that phrase for years, as I met expats in country after country.)

The expats were right that something was going on at the Cathedral of Santo Domingo, something big—a major demonstration. On my way from the apartment, I had been approached by a protester, accepted his brochure, and listened to a few speakers. The indigenous man with the microphone threw a fist into the air, shouting, "*Poder para la gente!*" My Spanish wasn't good enough to get the entire message, but the tone was clear. Anger needed no translation. Something about elections and disenfranchised, landless, indigenous peoples. Whatever it was, it was heating up.

When Leigh arrived, she'd heard rumors of discontent. "The last email before I left was from the conference organizers saying we might see political demonstrators at a distance, but they have nothing to do with the conference."

"At a distance, nothing doing," I said. "Those protestors are next-door to your conference location. You'll pass through them coming and going to meetings. No way you're going to ignore them."

"The email advised us to 'avoid any display of interest or sympathy', keep to our schedule, and go about our business."

How ironic that an international organization devoted to 'common land use' would ignore a rally for the disenfranchised literally next door. I said nothing. My daughter was a leftist rabble-rouser from her undergraduate days at Columbia and already into the protest scene at

Berkeley. I didn't want her to get started, particularly since I wasn't certain myself what was going on. For an entire week, Leigh and I walked past the cathedral, ignoring the posters, loudspeakers, and demonstrators. Pointedly, we looked away when we stopped for coffee in the café across the street, a spot that catered to foreigners.

Heavy-set, pigtailed Zapotec women sat on the curb not far from the chaos, weaving, babies on their backs or at their breasts, as the older children hawked their mothers' wares in the square. I bargained hard with one of the kids for a cotton shawl, which I got ridiculously cheap. Thinking about it later, I didn't much like myself and vowed to pay a fair price next time; sales were not a bargaining game for indigenous people, but their livelihood. Someone could organize those women, encourage a co-op, and show them how to work together rather than compete for customers. . . . Someone like me . . .

Instead, like an expat, I sat in coffee shops and read news of wealthy families' *quincineras* and scandals of the Mexican President's wife, implicated in fraudulent philanthropic practices.

Outside, demonstrators chanted from the square and Zapotecs begged on the corner.

While Leigh attended her conference, I went to Spanish school. On the first day, the Ugly American reared his head. Bermuda shorts, freckled knobby knees, red hair—he shouted, "I told the director she'd damned well better put me in one of those luxury homes. I want a private entrance, private bath with Jacuzzi, air-conditioning, and a big screen TV. Told her if she doesn't move me today, I'll cancel my payment, be outta here, badmouth her with a review."

At first I thought he was joking—who needed that kind of luxury at Spanish school?—but he was serious. He bragged he was going to 'immerse' in his fancy accommodation where he'd live with a 'typical' Mexican family. Remembering my language immersion in Nicaragua two years before—chickens, eleven people in a tiny house, one bathroom, two shifts at dinner—I didn't know whether to laugh or cry.

I couldn't pretend Oaxaca was an immersion for me; I'd taken Spanish as an excuse to spend time with my daughter. Days in Oaxaca passed in a haze of classes, art galleries, shopping, exquisite food, and an outing to the ancient ruins. Mornings, Leigh and I grabbed pastries at the cafe before going our separate ways. Afternoons, we lounged beside the pool with a Corona and later met friends from Spanish school for dinner. A culinary paradise, Oaxaca offered a feast for the palate, a different gourmet restaurant every night.

Leigh made her conference presentation and headed home to California. At the airport as she left, I berated myself for working so little on Spanish; in the next moment, however, I celebrated the precious and rare time with my daughter. Something important occurred to me standing there: outside of class, I hadn't had a single conversation with a Oaxacan since that first day in the park. Too much fun with Americans—an activity that would be routine if I were an expat. I determined not to make the same mistake in Puerto Escondido, where I would join the Habitat team to build.

From Oaxaca's cool mountains, I flew to the coast and a sweltering blanket of heat and humidity; it was crazy to build in Puerto Escondido in the summer. So focused on fleeing in August, I hadn't thought of hard labor in oppressive weather.

I checked into the *Flor de Mariá*, an oasis of cool tiles, potted ferns, a rooftop pool, private rooms with hot water baths. So different from my stifling accommodations with Habitat Nicaragua two years before—a dormitory and one cold-water bath for eight women. Maybe this was as 'modest' as it got in Puerto Escondido, a serious beach town. I was in heaven—two days to meander before the team arrived. Two days to ponder expats.

The scene at Zicatela Beach on the last day of an international surfing competition was a fifties beach-blanket movie. Male and female surfers, sleek bodies shiny with oil, strutted on the boardwalk, speaking mostly English as they ordered the locals around. I ate in a café owned by a Mexican woman and her American husband. "Mexican laws regarding beachfront ownership are convoluted," said the husband. "Only Mexican nationals may buy property outright within thirty miles of the beach. To sidestep the messy process of a trust required for foreigners, my wife 'owns' the cafe, but I'm the money behind it." Pointing to a hillside of new condos, he said, "Same for most of those, 'owned' by Mexicans on paper, but they belong to American expats."

After two days of cruising the town, drinking margaritas, shopping in the Frida Kahlo-crazy *tiendas,* and lazing in the pool, I was ready to work. The Habitat team arrived, and it was time to get serious.

First day of the build, I knew I'd leave Puerto Escondido with little connection to the homeowners. Much of the joy in Nicaragua two years before had been the relationship with the owners, the neighbors, and their kids—with us every day of the build. Our Mexican homeowner, Herlinda, was rarely on site, mostly passing through with no time to chat. Usually she was next door, inside her mother's house, with her sick baby. Her Navy husband was gone, and when he came home one day, he didn't visit the site or introduce himself. Since the only child was a baby, there were no neighborhood kids hanging around to play with or read to—the things we loved doing during breaks on the last build.

The interaction with locals was what I'd missed the week before in Oaxaca, and I was sure I'd have it on the build, but it was not to be. *Stop thinking of yourself,* I finally thought. *Whine, whine, it's not like Nicaragua. Get over it. You came to help a family, and so what if you're not going to become friends and have fun with kids. Focus on this great team and see what kind of good thing you can leave for these people who have so little and need so much.* And what a great team it was—seventeen to sixty-year-olds, Black and white, from a variety of states. We had breakfast together, walked to the building site, and worked until the sweat poured into our eyes. Afternoons, we raced to the hotel, dove into waves with our work clothes on, showered, and drank margaritas by the pool. As heterogeneous as we were, by Day Two we were a team.

Three days after arriving on site, we devised an alternative plan for truckloads of materials dumped daily way downhill from where they were needed. We couldn't efficiently continue to haul them uphill by the individual armful. Tom, an engineer by profession, got that crazed look engineering-types get when an idea strikes full force. "Look at all that stuff down there. Notice how long it takes us going up and down the hill, one by one, hauling up a load. There's a better way." Shovel in hand, Tom walked the hill, assessing the situation.

A half-hour later, Tom had dug the last of fifteen stair steps into the hill. He assigned each team member a spot, based on height and arm length. We formed a chain gang—fifteen *gringos*, stacked in order of height, tallest at the bottom of the hill—and passed up buckets of building materials. Tom, engineer that he was, kept a meticulous list of what we moved in five days:

4,000 bricks	5 lbs. Each	= 20,000 lbs.
500 cinderblocks	10 lbs. Each	= 5,000 lbs.
		25,000 lbs. 12.5 tons
sand		6.0 tons
rocks/gravel		4.8 tons

TOTAL   23.3 tons

And that didn't include the dirt we'd already hauled out, which added a couple more tons.

When I tell friends how much materials we move on a typical Habitat build, they are incredulous. "But why," someone always asks, "are you moving materials instead of building the house?" The reality is that tiny pieces of land where we often build Habitat houses are neither desirable nor accessible—often on a steep hillside or at the end of a long footpath or jammed wall-to-wall between two existing houses. Roads to building sites are rare, so when deliveries are made, the trucks may dump—and I mean, dump—the material in a messy pile of bricks or cinderblocks. The team hauls material to the site by wheelbarrow, bucket, blanket, or even on our heads. On the Mexico build, we became a bucket brigade, straight up a steep incline.
One day three pickup trucks pulled off the road below, drivers pointing excitedly. We had become a neighborhood sensation. One *señor* climbed the hill to ask how he could hire *la brigada* to help build his house. "*Hábitat Para La Humanidad,*" our leader explained, stressing that we were volunteers, as she summarized the program and gave him local contact information.
"*Muy bien.*" The man nodded, declared us *muy buenos trabajordores*, shook all our hands, and walked down the hill to rejoin his friends. The whole group, eight or so, looked up at us, raised their hands, and applauded. It's a

scene replayed at Habitat sites around the world—
communities flabbergasted that a bunch of Americans pay
to come to their country and volunteer to do manual labor
for someone they don't know.

Standing on the hill that day, I knew I was on to
something. The volunteer build hadn't been my primary
reason for coming to Mexico, but it was turning out to be
the most important. Grungy manual labor didn't exactly fit
my image of the expat life—eating, drinking, relaxing as I
had in Oaxaca, where I'd met only one local. Even if I
hadn't been close to the homeowners in Puerto Escondido,
I'd felt ties to the community. The neighbors knew we'd
been there, we'd made an impact, and left something
concrete.

Perhaps that's all anyone can hope for.

A conversation in town the next day sealed my fate.
I meandered into *el centro* to say goodbye to Gina, who
worked at the Information Booth. We'd become friendly
during the two weeks, practicing each other's languages,
and she knew I'd thought of living in Mexico.

"Tourists are pouring south along the Pacific
Coast," said Gina, "and we're getting ready for the boom.
You could have a job teaching English right now. In fact,
there's more than one job for you, so take your pick.
Resorts and condos are going up all around, the Americans
and Europeans are coming You could work for the city and
teach practical English to service people—waiters, taxi
drivers, hotel personnel. But with your degree, you might
want something more challenging with better pay, teaching
in the private high school. Lots of wealthy Mexicans live
here, and they want their children to learn good English
from a certified teacher. The school just lost its English
teacher, and the parents want someone"—she paused—
"more stable, not another new college grad." She meant the

parents wanted someone *older*, but she was too nice to say it.

"School starts in a few weeks. You could have that job, they'd hire you on the spot. Why don't you walk over there now and talk to them? Let me write the address."

Well, there it was. In my face. I could go home, tell my husband we were moving to Mexico, sell the house, get papers for the dog, get rid of all those things. Become an expat.

✎✎✎

Whom was I kidding? I wasn't going to do it. Yes, I was *free* from a fulltime job, but I wasn't totally free. I had a daughter on the opposite coast I wanted to see, an elderly mother in Assisted Living, a house, a husband, a dog, and a great part-time job. I would not join the drunken American in the Hotel Flor de Mariá. I would not join the look-alike couples drinking cocktails in the *zocalo* in Oaxaca. I would not join the foreign owners of luxury condos on the hillside above Zicatela beach.

I would not become an expat, that was certain. Little did I know, however, that the adventure in Mexico would set me on a path I would follow the rest of my life—volunteer travel. I was headed for countless adventures on five continents, in locales ranging from Madagascar to Mongolia, Bali to Bolivia. I would ride a camel in the Gobi, take a sleeper train across China, climb old Inca paths, catch a freighter to Patagonia, and roast marshmallows on a glowing volcano.

An expat? Why had I ever considered it?

Closet Closure by Sharon Canfield Dorsey
Chesapeake Bay Writers

Marie "somebody or other" took the country by storm by declaring we should only keep the things that "bring us joy." Everything else should go! When I heard that, my thought was, well, on a bad day, that could be a sloppy husband or a disobedient kid, or even the dog, when he chews up your favorite slippers. They are definitely not "bringing us joy" at that moment. There's also that other rule, "if you haven't used it in a year, off to the dump or the thrift store."

During a recent spring closet cleaning in my office, I discovered lots of things that should have been long gone under one or both of those rules:

…a small box of cassette tapes of my son's piano recital, age ten, and my daughter's performance in a speech contest, age twelve. He is now fifty and can only play chopsticks. She is forty-five and hates speaking in public. I can now play those tapes and say, "See, you should have kept practicing!"

…a box of old photos from the 70s of my Sweet Adeline barbershop chorus. Our show theme one year was "Fairy Tales," and we were all in different costumes depicting our favorite fairy tale, cartoon, or Disney character. I was in a tiny Wonder Woman costume that barely covered my 110 lb. skinny frame. Well, maybe that could have gone out. Today's comparison is depressing. Although, I am still trying to **be** Wonder Woman, just without the costume.

…a shoebox overflowing with old birthday and Christmas cards from people whose names I barely remember. Yes, I did look at every single one and I'm glad I did. Hidden among the throwaways, a birthday card from my grandfather the year he died. Tucked inside was a dollar bill. He sent one to each grandchild on every birthday, even after we'd grown up. ...two plastic storage boxes full of gloves and mittens with no mates. Maybe I thought they would find their way home someday? No joy there – gone!

...my high school and college yearbooks, certainly not used in a year or twenty-plus years. Do they bring me joy? Sure, remembering the friendships, the innocence, the fun; but joy tinged with sadness that so many of those friends are gone now. I received a note from a classmate the other day, saying, "We need to schedule a class reunion soon. We're dropping like flies!" I didn't know whether to laugh or cry.

...folders of yellowed newspaper clippings about celebrities, world events: Kennedy's assassination; Jane Fonda protesting the Vietnam War; planes flying into the Trade Center; an entire folder of stories about Elvis Presley's death. Yes, I did love him, I confess! Is there joy in those souvenirs of the past? Not exactly, but they **are** potent reminders of trials and tribulations we all survived together as a global community.

I have saved no clippings about the multitudes of people, worldwide, who have fallen victim to the coronavirus; the images of refrigerated trucks carrying their bodies away, sometimes to mass graves; the weary faces of health care heroes; the hungry, frightened faces of jobless millions. That pain is still too deep to be contained in a clipping.

I also haven't filed away stories about the recent racial protests or the horrendous video of George Floyd crying out for his mother as a policeman's knee forced the life from his body. I don't need clippings to recall that moment. The image is forever burned into my heart.

Someday, I trust, we will look back on these gut-wrenching experiences and be able to say we didn't just survive these latest trials and tribulations, but learned from them and stood with our brothers and sisters to bring about change. Those are the clippings I will save.

So, Marie, I opened a lot of doors to the past this week that wouldn't have been there if I'd listened to your advice. Those walks down memory lane brought me joy, some sadness, a little closure, but most importantly, the reassurance that this awful time, too, will pass.

Notes on images

Page 84, photos used under license from Creative Commons license 2.0 . Photographers Isaiah McClean (front left), David Hofmann (center back), & Hulki Okan Tabak (stage background)

Page 90, License under Creative Commons, 2.0

Page 96, Hula Doll

Page 100, Ballylooby Church of Our Lady and St. Kieran South Transept East Window SS. Paul and Luke 2012 09 08.jpg" by Andreas F. Borchert is licensed under CC BY-SA 4.0

Page 111, photo provided by Roger Tolle. "Sequenza III" by photographer Nat Tileston

Page 117, photo provided by Vivian Batts. Digital derivation by J. Nicolay

Page 120, digital derivation by J. Nicolay

Page 121, Hotel Flor de Mariá. Post card.

Page 134, derivative image by J. Nicolay

Teen Nib

Poetry

My Head is in an Oven by Ross Bazzichi
Teen Submission, First Place

My head is in an oven, my patience wearing thin.
My head is in an oven, no clue how I got in.
I just know I can't get out, no matter what I try.

Shouting,
Screaming,
Punching,
Kicking

Finally, my thoughts run dry.
Trapped inside that oven the heat begins to rise,
Almost in an instant, my brain begins to fry.
As the heat continues climbing, my tears, they turn to mist.
With your head trapped in an oven, one surely can't exist

4 Walls. 1 Window by Augustin Garcia
Teen Submission, Second Place

There are four walls and a window
Four walls and a window
4 walls. 1 window

There's a door too, but that's negligible
For all it matters, there could be four doors and a window
Doesn't matter. Negligible, remember?

Gray, white, white, white
Window on white

Now this window, this wonderful, gorgeous window-
Is falling apart. The insulation is tearing
The wind goes through and out the door
(It doesn't matter that the door is open, ignore it)
The screens held together by tape, poorly
Drapes drooping, devilishly dead

Doesn't open, doesn't close, doesn't do a window's thing
Unlike the door
(Ignore the door, for god's sake)-

This window, this wonderful, gorgeous window
A dash of purple, droplets of pink, sitting softly on sticks
Splotches of green, greener in the distance
Soothing fields of blue never to be touched

Oh, to be the birds that sing and fly and play
Oh, to be the birds that touch those fields
Oh, to be the birds that feel the wind firsthand
Oh, to be the birds that wake so early

Oh, to be the birds, so lucky and free

Needless to say,
This window should open
But it doesn't
The door, however-

Tic Toc Tic Toc
4 walls
Tic
1 window
Tic

Is a broken window simply a wall with a hole?
Tic

Feel the wind firsthand

Oh, to be a bird, so lucky and free
Oh, to be a bird, flying like me

An Accident in Three Parts by Mel Gross
Teen Submission, Third Place

"…a big, happy backyard full of flowers."

I. Grace Street

When we moved in nineteen years ago, it was
a rooming house. There was a kitchenette in the laundry
room,
a mattress in the foyer, & an orchestra
of crickets in the basement. The house was ninety years old
& not aging well.

My father winced at everything: the gas bill,
the water damage, the splintery floorboards. But my mother
saw past the peeling paint.
She called the rotted colonial columns
"good bones." She imagined color & curtains in place
of cobwebs. And most of all, she loved the wrap-around
porch.

It was an unbelievable investment. It was every penny
& more. It was a monstrosity.
But she loved that wrap-around porch.

So my father fixed everything. He patched
the walls, sanded the floors, laid down sod
in the backyard. He even built
the stairs. You can tell how much he loved her
just by walking up the stairs.

II. The New House

It was an accident—we weren't ready
to move. But when that blue-tiled bathroom & the cup
of its perky little bathtub came into view, my mother & I
paused
together in the hallway, and we just knew.

Of course, my father still had to be sold on it, and he's not
an easy man to convince. But he heard the delighted spread
of my mother's laugh in the kitchen. He saw the expression
on her face. And he just knew.

So they took out a bridge loan &
crossed their fingers hard &
bought that little house
across the city.

III. Better Bones
The new house across the city
has a big, happy backyard full of flowers
that my mother calls "weeds." It has a big
cracked concrete stoop & a big
ugly knocker on the front door. Best
of all, it has a little blue room just for me, flooded—& I
mean
absolutely flooded—with light.

Fiction

Why Lyon Kaltz was late by Sara Acevedo-Bonilla
Teen Submission, First Place

Lyon Kaltz's classmates waited every morning for Lyon to be late. He would always tell a story on why he was late, and for many of the students in classroom 306, it was what really woke them up in the morning. They would then go to their parents and siblings and repeat Lyon's story. Lyon's teacher was constantly waiting for the day his excuse could be proven a lie. Often the story included why he did not have his homework, which made the teacher even more determined to prove him wrong. Many don't know how, but something would always happen that would prove his story true. Most just supposed he just had the best luck in the world. Today, however, Lyon was especially late to class, and his classmates were fidgeting in their seats awaiting his arrival. Finally, just as the clock hit 8:45 a.m., Lyon burst into the classroom. His brown, moppy hair was wet despite the sunshine outside and his clothes were damp, with his shoes making a squishy noise. The students' glance at each other, waiting for the show to begin. The teacher clucks her tongue, showing her disapproval.

"Late again, Mr. Kaltz," the teacher slithers. Lyon looks at his teacher with a wide look.

"Oh, Mrs. McLaren, you won't believe what just happened," Lyon says with a glint in his eye.

His classmates start smiling, ignoring the work in front of them.

"I'm sure I won't. Why are you late Mr. Kaltz?" asked Mrs. McLaren with a raised eyebrow. Lyon takes a deep breath.

"Well, Mrs. McLaren, I woke up and started getting ready extra early so I would not be late for school. Once I was ready to go, I said goodbye to my parents and hopped on my bike. After only two minutes in my ride school, I had to hit the brakes on my bike because there was a cow in my way. I almost hadn't seen it, because I was enjoying the scenery. The cow stood in the middle of the road while munching on something. I didn't want to go around it and leave it alone in the middle of the road because I didn't want anyone to accidentally hit the cow with their car. So, I got off my bike and started trying to move it. I pushed it hard again and again, but it would not budge. I tried pushing on its side, then I tried pushing from behind, but the cow would not move! Then I tried yelling really loudly and jumping to scare it, but it just looked at me with a bored look. I decided to get my parents' help, so I rode my bike back to the house, but my parents had already left the house. I got back on my bike and rode back, but the cow was gone! I looked around, trying to find it, but it was nowhere in sight. At this point, I checked my watch and saw that I could still get to school on time if I tried, so I got back on my bike and started riding. I decided to try and take a shortcut, but when I turned around the corner of the street…" Lyon pauses for dramatic effect, thrusting his arms out, "there was the cow, and it looked like it got all its friends because there were about thirty more cows behind her. I tried to go back but there was one behind me and I accidentally rode on its tail. It mooed super loudly. All of the other cows looked at me with a creepy look, so I went around the one behind me and started riding away. Then all of the cows started mooing super loudly and I heard a loud sound behind me. Without looking back I could tell they were coming after me. I started pedaling harder, trying to get away, but cows are faster than I thought. I kept riding and zigzagging, but I could not lose them. Then I had an idea: if I went towards Main Street, they would get scared with all the cars and stop chasing me. So I went in that direction. When I cut through the main street, cars started honking. I went through the park and looked behind me, but the cows weren't there.

"Grinning with victory, I looked ahead just in time to see a pond right in front of me. I tried to stop and put the break on my front wheel but all that did was fling me into the lake. My foot got stuck in the bottom mush of the pond and I almost drowned! Thankfully, my foot got unstuck and I was able to swim back to the top." Lyon looks at his teachers with an innocent look, "I lost my bookbag in the pond. Sadly, my homework was in my bookbag. I tried to swim back down to the bottom of the pond to find my bookbag, but I couldn't find it. So, I got out of the pond and got back on my bike. Looking at my watch again, I realized I was now late for school. So, I started riding towards school. Just as school was in sight, I heard a loud noise that can only be explained by a herd of cows. The cows found me! Determined to make it to school, I pedaled harder. Just as the cows were gaining on me, I hopped off my bike and ran into the school. Then I ran as fast as I could and got here to the classroom," Lyon finishes panting. His classmates look up to their teacher to see her reaction. Mrs. McLaren frowns, wrinkling her nose.

Mrs. McLaren asks, "Mr. Kaltz, how do you expect me to believe this story? It is absolutely ridiculous." Lyon shrugs and opens his mouth to speak, but just as he does the loudspeaker of the school turns on.

The principal barks, "There will be no recess outside today. We are having a cow situation and we want no children hurt."

Lyon's classmate's grin, suppressing laughter. Mrs. McLaren frowns, annoyed that once more luck was on Lyon's side.

"Sit down, Mr. Kaltz. No need to interrupt my class any longer." She says as she turns to face the class.

Smiling wide Lyon walks to his desk nodding hello to his classmates the whole way. After he sits down all the students in classroom 306 prepare to wait another day to hear another adventurous excuse for why Lyon Kaltz is late.

The Florist by Cara J. Hadden
Teen Submission, Second Place

I have always loved flowers. They remind me of my mother. She taught me that a well-cared for flower can comfort a lost soul or mend a broken heart. I just wish flowers could explain the visions.

I was about seven when they started. My mother took me to her 'office'—a small flower cart permanently stationed just off Main Street—and sat me down on the curb while she sold flowers to tourists and husbands in trouble with their wives. My brown hair waving in the wind, I watched people step into stores and leave with crinkly plastic bags. It was then that I made eye contact with an old man in a black suit about to cross the street. My head went fuzzy, and in my mind's eye I saw the man in the same suit, but younger and happier. He was dancing with a woman in a white dress with sweet pea flowers braided into her blonde hair. As the man twirled her, the woman looked at me and pulled a pink sprig from her head. She then pressed the flower into my hand and whispered, "Tell him I had to say goodbye." With a wide smile, the woman returned to her loving husband before finishing the dance with a dip.

The vision dissipated as quickly as it appeared. Once again finding myself on the edge of the curb, I glimpsed the old man shaking his head and stepping onto the crosswalk. Filled with an odd sense of purpose, I grabbed a sweet pea flower from my mother's cart while she talked to a customer and ran after him.

I caught up to him on the other side of the street and tugged at his jacket to get his attention. His eyes widened in shock when he saw what I was holding.

"Who—what—why do you have this?" the man spluttered.

"The lady in white that was dancing with you told

me to tell you she had to say goodbye," I said, raising the plant closer to his face.

Tears pooled in the man's eyes as he took the flower. "My wife wore this in her hair when we got married. It was the happiest day of my life." He sniffed. "I buried her today."

"Maybe that's why she wanted you to have a goodbye flower."

The man silently broke into a smile and hugged me, his hands shaking. "Thank you, little one. Thank you." When he let me go, he gave me a five-dollar bill and placed the pink flower in his lapel before walking away with a lighter step.

I never told my mother about the vision. Or the dozens after that. Frankly, I did not understand them enough to know how to tell her. But over time, whenever I viewed a piece of someone's life connected to a flower, it almost always led to more business for Mom. She never discovered my secret power, but I could tell she was proud of me.

Fifteen years passed, and eventually, so did Mom. When I took over her flower cart, the visions became more frequent, but selling flowers kept her close to my heart.

One humid summer day, I was putting up an umbrella over my cart to protect the plants from the heat when I saw a young woman carrying a toddler with ginger hair. They were wearing threadbare sweatshirts, and the toddler looked like he had not bathed in a long time. As I made eye contact with the mother, the world went fuzzy, and in my mind's eye I saw the woman wearing an elegant gown in a hotel room. The bathroom door opened to reveal what appeared to be an adult version of the redheaded toddler wearing a tuxedo and a medal depicting the profile of Alfred Nobel. The woman all but flew to her son and hugged him tightly before he presented his mother with a bouquet of pink carnations.

I was jolted back to reality the moment the mother walked past my cart. One of the colorful plants must have caught his eye, because the little boy pointed in my direction and yelled, "Pretty!"

The mother turned to the flowers and said softly to her son, "I don't have money for flowers, sweetie." The toddler grew fussy when she walked away.

"Wait, ma'am!" I grabbed a pink carnation off my cart and caught up to the woman. "I couldn't help but notice your son liked my flowers."

The son clapped his hands with a smile, but the mother scowled at me like I was about to steal her kid. "He's, um, allergic to pollen, so he can't be near flowers." Her eyes darted from side to side before shuffling around me, the little boy now starting to cry.

"That's too bad," I said before she was out of earshot. "This particular flower is for free today."

Seemingly against her better judgement, the woman hurried back to my side, plucked the flower from my hand and placed it in her son's. His smile was bright enough to light outer space. "Thanks, lady. I think you made his day."

I shook my head. "No, you did. A pink carnation symbolizes a mother's love. If you keep doing what you're doing for him, he'll accomplish great things one day. I know it."

The expression the woman gave me all but telegraphed that she thought I was nuts. "Ok, lady. Thanks again."

You won't think I'm crazy in twenty-five years," I said under my breath, the toddler waving goodbye while his mother turned the corner.

I returned to my cart to find a handsome man standing in the shade of my umbrella, talking on his phone.

He looked around my age, wearing a t-shirt and blue Bermuda shorts that clashed with his dirty blond hair.

I stepped behind my cart just as he ended his phone call, and when we unintentionally locked eyes, the world quaked with a violent ferocity. In my mind's eye, I saw the man lying in a field of red roses, seemingly asleep. After a moment, he sat up and stared at me with cornflower blue eyes and smiled like he had seen the sun rise over the horizon. In the vision, I felt myself lay down next to him, and he reached over to pick a rose just above my head. "A rose for my Rosie," he said before he gave me the flower and kissed me gently on the lips. I felt a sharp pain—the thorns were digging into my hand—but I didn't care so long as I was with him.

"Did you see that?" The man under the umbrella asked me when I grabbed my cart for support until my head stopped spinning.

"Of course, I saw that I always see stuff like that, but—." I did a double take as his words set in my foggy mind. "Wait, you saw it too? That's never happened before."

"The field, you, me, the roses. And—oh, you're bleeding." He gestured to my right hand, which was dripping blood from wounds that could only be from rose thorns. "Is this, uh, normal for you?"

"Kind of." I wrapped my hand with some paper towels from under the cart. "I get visions a lot, usually scenes from other people's lives that involve flowers, but no one else has ever seen one of my visions before. And I've certainly never been hurt before." I knew I was rambling, but the man's blue eyes shattered my composure, and I could not stop myself.

"Wow." He looked completely dumbfounded, grasping for words not yet there. "And do these visions come true?"

"So far, yes. Besides, the subjects of my visions

often become good customers, so I can't complain." I immediately cringed. "I promise I'm not a scam artist, I just see things I can't control so I try to make up for it by giving flowers to people who need them."

The man laughed. "Don't worry, I believe you. I saw you with that mother earlier. It's inspiring how you bring people joy." He cleared his throat awkwardly. "Well, since this vision is bound to come true, I should probably introduce myself. I'm Hunter."

My hand throbbed a little as blood rushed to my cheeks. "I'm Rosie. Nice to meet you."

"I don't suppose I could buy you a rose, Rosie?"

I smiled. "Sure, what color?"

"Red?"

I raised an eyebrow. "It's the color of love, but rather expensive. Are you sure?"

He held my injured hand and lightly kissed it. "If I truly saw a glimpse of our future, then it's worth it."

It has been five years since my last vision. It's also been five years since Hunter and I married. My mother was right. Under the right caretaker, a flower can bring joy, peace, and love to anyone willing to accept such a simple gift.

Stone Smiles by Autumn Ryan
Teen Submission, Third Place

The air felt empty. She heard no wind, no shouts from children playing in a distant field, no birds singing in the trees above; even the leaves beneath her feet, sodden with that morning's rain, were silent. Her mind was the same. The echoes of arguments that usually bombarded her on these walks did not come, even as she contemplated that fact. Her thoughts were wordless, and her feet moved on instinct.

She admired the trees around her. Looking at them, her sense of solitude felt rather ironic: These trees were alive, and had they been able to move she would've been in the midst of a bustling crowd. And yet, she felt utterly alone. But the trees were not what she came for.

At the end of her path lay a cliff just high enough, with slick black rocks below just hard enough, to strike her with grateful oblivion should she jump. But that is not what she came for, either.

Beyond the trees, and beyond the cliff, there were mountains. Rounded by age, their slopes were so smooth that she could imagine sliding down one like a child on a playground. The sheer size of them held her in awe, but there was more to them than that. Their already soft-looking surfaces were made fuzzy by thick layers of moss painting the dark backdrop with bright shades of blue, yellow, and peach, like streaks from a giant's paintbrush. It was easy to let her mind wander, and she gave in to imagination's sweet escape.

She could see the giant (made of gray stone crisscrossed with jade vines) carelessly streaking the landscape with springy pastels. When he finished, his chair - a solid plateau jutting from five conjoined peaks - sat ready. She watched as he absent-mindedly brushed some brown, oily-looking birds from its surface. They squawked in complaint. The giant caught sight of her and gave a gentle smile before bending to sip from a spring. The birds settled on his broad shoulders, and the quiet stillness of this imaginary world returned, and remained - until it was interrupted by, of all things, wind chimes.

She looked around, only vaguely aware of the reality that still surrounded her. She had hiked for miles, and there were not any houses around. A quick search for their source revealed a rope ladder just feet from her right arm.

She jumped. Of all the times she'd been down this path, she'd never noticed it. But there it was, swinging lazily over the deadly cliff and back as if there were nothing wrong with its existence. As if it belonged there, just like the clumsy-looking treehouse it hung from. A brown bird squawked from its roof.

"What the..." A breeze stole her words. Once again, she moved instinctually, this time towards the ladder. She wrapped her hands around the rung just above her head, then began to climb.

It was as if reality hit her the second her feet left the ground. The ladder was as careless as ever, swinging smoothly towards the precipice. A sudden gust of wind from behind didn't help. The ladder's smooth motion became urgent, and it rushed forwards until it was too late for her to let go. She watched the ground escape from behind her until she was nearly parallel to it. The ladder paused.

She lay on nothing but air, clinging uselessly to this loosely tied bundle of ropes, the origins of which she had no idea. And yet, she had trusted them with her life. All it would take was just one slip of a hand or foot, and she would be falling, staring at...

The sky was beautiful. She saw it as clearly as if she was laying in an open field. Its blue was richer than she knew possible, and ordinary clouds would have seemed yellow in comparison to the pristine white of the ones in that moment. The sun would have been painfully bright had the cool afternoon shadow of the trees not reached her.

Unfortunately, she only had a moment to appreciate this before the ladder began its hasty return.

Her descent seemed much faster than her approach. And, whereas before she could save herself by clinging to the ladder, she was now headed straight for a tree. If she'd had more time to think, she would have realized that the top of the ladder wouldn't swing quite as far; if she climbed a few rungs higher, she'd have walked away with only a bruised behind. Or perhaps if she just let go of the ladder as it swung back over the cliff, the leaves would have been a more forgiving cushion. But she could not process either thought before the forest echoed with the crack of bone on solid wood.

She awoke to disappointment. The magnificent blue of the sky had faded to a lackluster excuse for a sunset: dingy orange, like a prison jumpsuit. The rope ladder still swung lazily above her. Upon closer inspection, she noticed one of the rungs was missing, which explained the frayed piece of rope she clutched in her right hand. *Strange*, she thought, having no memory of the ladder breaking. She attributed her confusion to the head trauma she suffered, then stood.

One of the oily brown birds she had seen on the giant's shoulders stood before her, tilting its head curiously. It was larger up close, its beak fist sized. It stretched its wings, then glanced over the cliff. It looked back at her meaningfully.

She crept to the edge. The giant's massive stone hand waited for her just below the precipice. Below the hand was the giant's face, greeting her with the same warm smile as before. She felt the bird's greasy wing press against her, urging her to step down. It squawked, then hopped onto one of the fingers. She followed.

As the giant's hand descended, the brown bird flapped its massive wings and returned to the cliff. She watched it peer down at her as she came closer to the moss that had fascinated her for years. The fuzzy covering seemed to wave in greeting, moving as if it were made of many small parts instead of being one thick mat of plant. The giant paused a few feet from the surface. She was close enough to jump but wasn't sure if she should; one glance at the giant's amiable smile told her not to worry. She took a few steps back, then leapt.

Her feet landed on the moss. She did not hear the soft thud of an object on carpet like she expected, but instead the unmistakable crunch of hundreds of exoskeletons. A squelch not unlike sticking a spoon into a new jar of jelly followed. The moss began to crawl up her legs. Its thousands - looking farther, probably billions - of tiny pincers flashed in the dwindling sun.

The bird lingered a moment, then flew away.

The Sycamore Gazette
May 28, 2020

When witnesses reported hearing a single gunshot from Euqseakfak Forest two weeks ago, police expected to arrest a poacher. They searched for less than an hour before leaving, promising the area's residents they would return if it became an issue. When no further reports were made, the incident was forgotten.

Forgotten, that is. except by local resident and acknowledged local "nature guardian" Jay Brown. He claims to be one of the original witnesses.

"I knew right away somebody was messing with my woods," he remarked to us in an interview on Friday.

"When I heard the police just gave up, I took it on myself to protect that forest."

Two days after the incident, Brown found himself wandering through trees, not sure what he was looking for until he found it.

He told our interviewer, "After I looked in all the popular hunting spots … I decided to check the pretty trail. It leads to this nice overlook over Figment Lake. I really did not want to find anything there, because if I did, something weird would be going on. But I found something."

What did he find? "A trail of small footprints. Probably from a young lady," Brown suggested.

That led him straight down the little-used trail to an even stranger sight: a piece of frayed rope laying on the ground.

"I have no idea where it came from," he admitted, "but the rest of it's probably over the cliff." He reasoned that since there was only one line of footprints, whoever made them did not return.

Brown relayed this to police, but they have yet to  act. Speculations arose connecting this strange occurrence to the case of a teen girl who disappeared just hours before the gunshot. Police labelled her a runaway; a decision police are unlikely to change. It seems both mysteries are a long way from being solved. The only comfort that we at the Sycamore Gazette can offer the community is a comment from our citizen hero, Jay Brown, "There's no body below that cliff. I made sure of it myself."

Nonfiction

Ancestors by Patience Wallace
Teen Submission, First Place

I clutch my bookbag to my chest, trapped by my mother's angry gaze. Her lips are pointed, her dark brown eyes are nearly boiling; she is mad. My stomach starts to flip, realizing I've gotten myself in trouble.

"Did you sit in the back today?" mom growls, daring me to challenge her.

"Yes?" I am confused, how did she know I was

sitting in the back?

"What have I told you about sitting in the back," she yells.

"Well, all my friends sit in the back, I don't want to sit up in the front with the kindergarteners! People will make fun of me!"

"Would you rather be made fun of or get in trouble?"

Rather get in trouble, I think. "Be made fun of," I reply. "How'd you even see me sitting in the back?

"When I saw you walking all the way from the back of the bus when I picked you up from your stop. You know better! What have I told you about this, do you not think about Rosa Parks?"

No, not really, I think. A painting of her hangs over the loveseat in the living room. Her light brown face surrounded by the warm yellows of a public bus, the purple dark leather of the bus seat stark against her light pink tweed jacket. Her hair is frizzy, a slash of white through the black strands, her lips set in a straight line, the light bouncing off her glasses. I do not really care about her, she died in 1960 or something.

"You should know what she went through so your black butt can sit in the front! And what do you do? Sit in the back like we were forced to do!" I stare at my mom blankly. Yeah, we were forced to do it, but that was a long time ago; now we can sit wherever we want. But no respectable fourth grader would be caught dead sitting with the little kids. I briefly think about Martin Luther King Jr., one of the three black role models I had been taught about, including Harriet Tubman and Rosa Parks.

"People died so you can sit in the front. You're disrespecting our ancestors! You should be ashamed of yourself!"

What? I think. Disrespecting my ancestors?

"If you were smart, you'd find it in your best interest to sit in the front." She moves and I flinch, squinting my eyes as I prepare to be hit. The hit does not come, but her thick fingers pluck me, a quick pinpoint of pain in the middle of my forehead. I instinctively rub the spot, my facial expression turning sour.

"Fix your face." She stares at me for a minute, seemingly deciding whether she would punish me or not. "This time, you're getting a pass, but if I see you sitting in the back again, you're getting in trouble." My eyes bubble with tears, biting my lip to keep from crying; but I manage to give her a small smile.

"Yes ma'am." I nod quickly, putting down my bookbag as she turns away, not wanting her to see me cry.

The next day I sit in the middle of the bus, not daring to go all the way to the back and risk getting caught. I would turn around and yell at my friends through what felt like 50 rows of seats, complaining to them at lunch about my crazy mother and my "ancestors." We all laughed about it like it was not true. Like we had not felt less than because of our blackness. Like we had not been treated differently than our white counterparts. Like we had not feared for our brothers and fathers' lives. Like we did not know about the feeling of deep-rooted shame we were born with, just because of the amount of melatonin in our skin.

It wasn't till I saw the freedom riders, dark smoke billowing from the windows, till I saw the skeleton of a bus being put out, till I could imagine the panic in the bus as people burned to death. It was not till I saw the bloated face of Emmett Till, leached of all signs of humanity. Until I saw Martin Luther King Jr., the man with a dream, lying in a coffin.

Listening from Behind the Counter by Lillian Lam
Teen Submission, Second Place

Sometimes kids do not understand how hard their parents work to provide for them. I always felt upset when my parents never showed up to any school events, like band concerts. I could not participate in any activities outside of school because my parents never have time to drive me. You see, my parents owned a restaurant, and they must work every day of the week to help support their family.

They would spend all day working from the time they get up to late at night, and I would help after school by being a cashier. I was always taught that you can learn about the world from any job by listening to others, which listening to customers' stories helped me realize. Despite having only a glimpse into other people's lives, I have learned so much about diversity and human connections. Perhaps being a cashier is not anything special and it also is not the best job, but it can help you realize how unique every individual is.

People from all stages of life come to the restaurant, and some share their experiences with me. There are parents who come in with newborns barely a week old. Love and excitement of becoming a new parent is always a beautiful sight, and parents who adopt also have the same look in their eyes. I have met a family who experienced transracial adoptions, and the love for their child is the same. These parents spend a lot of time trying to incorporate the child's original culture with their own. Sometimes parents bring in toddlers, which are sometimes difficult to handle. They run around while the parents try to calm them down, but it is all in good fun when they wave me goodbye. Families come in all shapes and sizes, and once there were parents who came in with seven children by their side. Kids are truly a gift of innocence and a blessing in people's lives.

Teenagers are a common sight because they appear

in groups when school is out. They talk among themselves, and sometimes they know me from behind the counter. Some stop by to say hello while others come in without a word before leaving awkwardly out the door. Parents of some teens will drop them off at the front door to pick up their food. The purpose is for the teens to learn how to pay for their own things with cash or a credit card. However, it is not always easy when dealing with teenagers because there are times when they do not realize the rudeness of their actions. Many times, parents come in talking about how much they worry about their child's future. They talk about teens getting in trouble with the law, smoking at home, and throwing their hard work in school away. These parents usually tell those stories to receive comfort and teach a lesson to me so that I do not make the same mistakes.

The workforce comes afterwards, and some students join the workforce while others go for higher education. I have met people from all parts of the workforce. Sometimes there are people that are homeless and without a job. They come in to pay with coins, and to say some wise words about reality. They talk about their mistakes and how they are just finding their way through life. These people make my heart ache as I wish them a nice day. Others work in labor-intensive jobs, such as irons mines and construction work. They usually come in with dirtied hands that are black as coal from working on dusty ground. Once a man came in to give me a heavy rock to show the iron formation. Another came in, quite malnourished, talking about how he spends his days placing asphalt on roads. These people talk about their long work hours and the pain of having such demanding jobs. I have learned so much about these jobs from the workers, who have mobility problems and sometimes walk with a limp.

There are people that come in from higher paid jobs. Teachers are one example, and some are the ones that taught me in the past. There are people with jobs like me, a cashier, and complain about rude customers from their long day. Office workers appear right after work in Polo shirts and dead looks in their eyes. Military workers arrive in uniform and the nation's pride. They are all waiting to return home to their families, the happiness in their lives. Some people are more accomplished, owning a large business. With expensive cars and clothes, they seem to have a league of their own. Most would think that the wealthy would act snobby and pretentious, but the ones I know are kind, down to Earth, and have bright smiles on their faces. I have also talked to people from all parts of STEM: nurses, doctors, engineers, programmers, and scientists in all fields of science. Scientists that are biologists, NASA scientists, chemists, and environmentalists. Conversations with people from all parts of the workforce helps me understand each occupation's strengths and weaknesses. Ultimately, these chats will help me in deciding the right job for my own future.

Diversity blooms where people least expect. A restaurant allows people of all unique differences to meet and interact. Races and ethnicities do not have a boundary in small business because they are all seen as customers that I can befriend and serve. I have conversed with people that trace back from different parts of the world. People all have a ethnicity that they identify as: Indian, Korean, Chinese, African-American, Irish, Russian, German, Filipinos, Mexicans, and many more that I cannot possibly name. Every person has their own culture, and they tell me about some of their traditions. Even though I cannot meet people from every culture in the world, I can still learn about diversity from the different people that talk to me. A person's skin does not identify who someone is, and I have met someone who had vitiligo and talked to me about the condition. Gender and sexuality also do not have a boundary because I've talked to people that are gay, lesbian, transgender, and many more. People have differences but are equal because they are all humans.

I have learned so much from talking to the older generation and people with health problems. There was a customer who changed his lifestyle because he survived a heart attack. There are customers who battled cancer and are grateful for life. A man I have met had larynx cancer and uses an Electrolarynx to talk to me. There is an elderly woman who always wears a nasal cannula because of respiratory problems, and I deliver the woman's order right to her car. Some elderly people have high spirits and tell jokes to get some laughs. However, many people live in nursery homes and are waiting for a family member to visit. They talk about their new grandchildren and how proud they are of their children. Conversations are about how much one visit from family means to them, and these people tell me that I need to visit my parents when I become an adult. Having a family member die without a visit will cause regret that will last in a lifetime. Even one surprise visit can let one person die with peace in his or her mind.

People do not realize how connected their lives are at a local scale. A simple job of a cashier can connect me to people that are different in unimaginable ways. To take the time to listen, to watch, and to understand the stories of customers can make a big difference in a person's understanding of society. It makes someone more understanding of differences and more open-minded on issues that are local and global. Talking to different people allows for different perspectives on a topic and shows the similarities and differences of people's beliefs from different generations. I always felt that being a cashier wasn't a good or a 'cool' job, but now I think that it is truly a blessing to have this job and learn about the local community and the diversity in it.

Despite many people having differences that makes them seem distant from one another, they can all be connected under something as little as a cashier. Everyone that has talked to me are connected to me and each other because they are all customers and people that shared their experiences with a teen. Some people that come in are children of people who are customers when the restaurant was first opened. Others are new and just moved into the area, and many have watched me grow up from a baby to a cashier. I'm grateful for my parents for allowing to learn via this job and to the customers that share their experiences with me. One thing is for sure: people can be connected by something small such as a restaurant, a smile, and some words.

Apollo 13: The Successful Failure by Alyssa Kitts
Teen Submission, Third Place

President John F. Kennedy challenged NASA to join the Space Race and in doing so he instituted America's greatest achievement due to his strong desire to beat the Russians. NASA accepted the challenge and soon launched a man to the moon. While Apollo missions were major accomplishments for NASA, the Apollo 13 mission is considered the "most successful failure" because of the crew's quick observations of the problem and the determination of the experts in Houston's Command Center to solve the problem.

President John F. Kennedy was determined to win the Space Race because Russia was much farther along. By 1957 Russia had already launched the first living creature into space, a dog named Laika. Also, in 1965 Alexei Leonov became the first person to walk in space. The first attempted mission for the United States' Apollo program, Apollo 1, was a failure. During the on-ground flight test, the ship door got stuck and the men couldn't get out. The three astronauts on the ship died in the fire.

So NASA decided to take it slow and the next 5 missions were unmanned. Apollo missions 2 through 6 were unmanned flight tests to find out how they could get astronauts into space safely and then get them back home. Apollo 2 through 6 went up into space without any astronauts and collected data about how to keep them alive. Apollo 2 studied weightlessness, and Apollo 3 tested navigation and guidance systems. Apollo 4 worked on the heat shield, and Apollo 5 and 6 worked on re-entry and the possibility that man can live in space.

Apollo 7 was the first manned mission. On October 11, 1968, Apollo 7 took flight. It did not quite get to the moon but orbited around Earth. On December 21, 1968 Apollo 8 was launched, this mission was able to orbit the moon ten times. It was also the first manned mission to enter lunar orbit. Apollo 9 got to orbit the earth 152 times and was sent up to demonstrate rendezvous and docking. Apollo 10 was able to orbit the moon for the second time in NASA history. In 1969 Neil Armstrong the Apollo 11 Commander made history by being the first person to walk on the moon and made his famous quote, "One small step for man one giant leap for mankind." We had won the Space Race and beat the Russians. Apollo 12 was the 2nd mission to land on the moon. Then came Apollo 13.

On April 11, 1970, Apollo 13 launched. During the launch, the center engine shutdown, but this did not affect the mission. On the ship on April 13th with the quick observations of the crew, Apollo 13 was saved. The astronauts thought they had felt a hit to the ship, then Commander Jim Lovell noticed fumes coming from the side of the ship and quickly alerted Houston's Control Center. Apollo 13 was headed for the Fra Mauro area on the moon, but all of that changed when they found out the oxygen tank had exploded at 10:07 p.m. on April 13th.

Turns out Beech, the tank manufacturer, failed to change the 25 volt heater switch to a 65 volt like it was supposed to. Also the oxygen tank had been dropped 5 years earlier and no one had noticed that the vent tube was out of alignment. They had the risk of losing air and the ship could easily go off course.

Before Apollo 13 took flight, people wondered

about the mission because it was set to launch at the 13th minute of the 13th hour on April 11, 1970. NASA did not pay attention to all of the fuss and continued the mission anyway. Then during liftoff, the center engine broke down, but that was only the beginning. Then on April 13th while in space, the O2 tank exploded. After the explosion they had to use the moon's orbital stream to throw them around the moon and launch them back to Earth. This gave them the record of being the farthest mission away from Earth. Jack Swigert the Command Module Pilot, who unfortunately died of inoperable lung cancer in 1982, oversaw getting the Odyssey back safe and sound, with the help of Fred Haise the Lunar Module Pilot, and Commander Jim Lovell. The mission was a success and they achieved splashdown on April 17th at 1:07 pm.

The Houston Command Center was a big part of the Apollo 13 mission accomplishment.

They produced a solution about the oxygen dilemma, and they played a major part in getting Apollo 13 home. The Command Center helped them design a filter made of simple tools onboard to suck in the carbon dioxide so they would have more oxygen. The Command Center also figured out how to get them home safely. They figured out that the crew would have to use the moon's orbital stream to launch them back to Earth. The Command Center had a hard time figuring out a solution because of how little power they had left in the ship.

In conclusion, the Apollo program was successful. All it took was one footprint of the Commander of Apollo 11, Neil Armstrong to step on the moon to win the Space Race and beat the Russians. President John F. Kennedy gave the American people a goal of reaching the moon, an achievement for which the American people should be proud. While the Apollo missions were great accomplishments for NASA, the Apollo 13 mission was known as the "most successful failure" because of the crew's quick observations of the problem and the determination of the experts in Houston's Command Center to solve the problem and because no one died - the astronauts returned to Earth safely.

Fred Haise, John Swigert, and James Lovell. Image credit: NASA.

Notes on images

Page 137, all images, unless otherwise noted are in the public domain. "Boy in oven"

Page 139, ramshackle house with bird

Page 142, image provided by J. Nicolay

Page 143, cows chasing boy on bike

Page 151, image provided by Cara J. Hadden

Page 156, image provided by Autumn Ryan

Page 157, sketch by J. Nicolay

Page 158, Rose Parks, thumbnail, setting fair use, public domain by J. Nicolay

Page 162, illustration by J. Nicolay

Page 170, Fred Haise, John Swigert, and James Lovell. Image credit: NASA